5

'the underlying intention is to reaffirm the basic principles of Italian gastronomy: freshness, simplicity and lack of pretension.'

STEFANOdePIERI

modern italian food

Photography by Earl Carter

Hardie Grant Books

To Alison

With gratitude
to all my staff.

This edition published in 2006
First published in 2004
by Hardie Grant Books
85 High Street
Prahran, Victoria 3181, Australia
www.hardiegrant.com.au

Cataloguing-in-Publication Data is available from the
National Library of Australia.

ISBN 10: 1-74066-436-1
ISBN 13: 978-1-74066-436-3

Photography by Earl Carter
Cover and text design by Guy Mirabella
Typeset by Pauline Haas, Girl's Own Graphics
Props courtesy of Minimax
Printed and bound in China by SNP Leefung

10 9 8 7 6 5 4 3 2 1

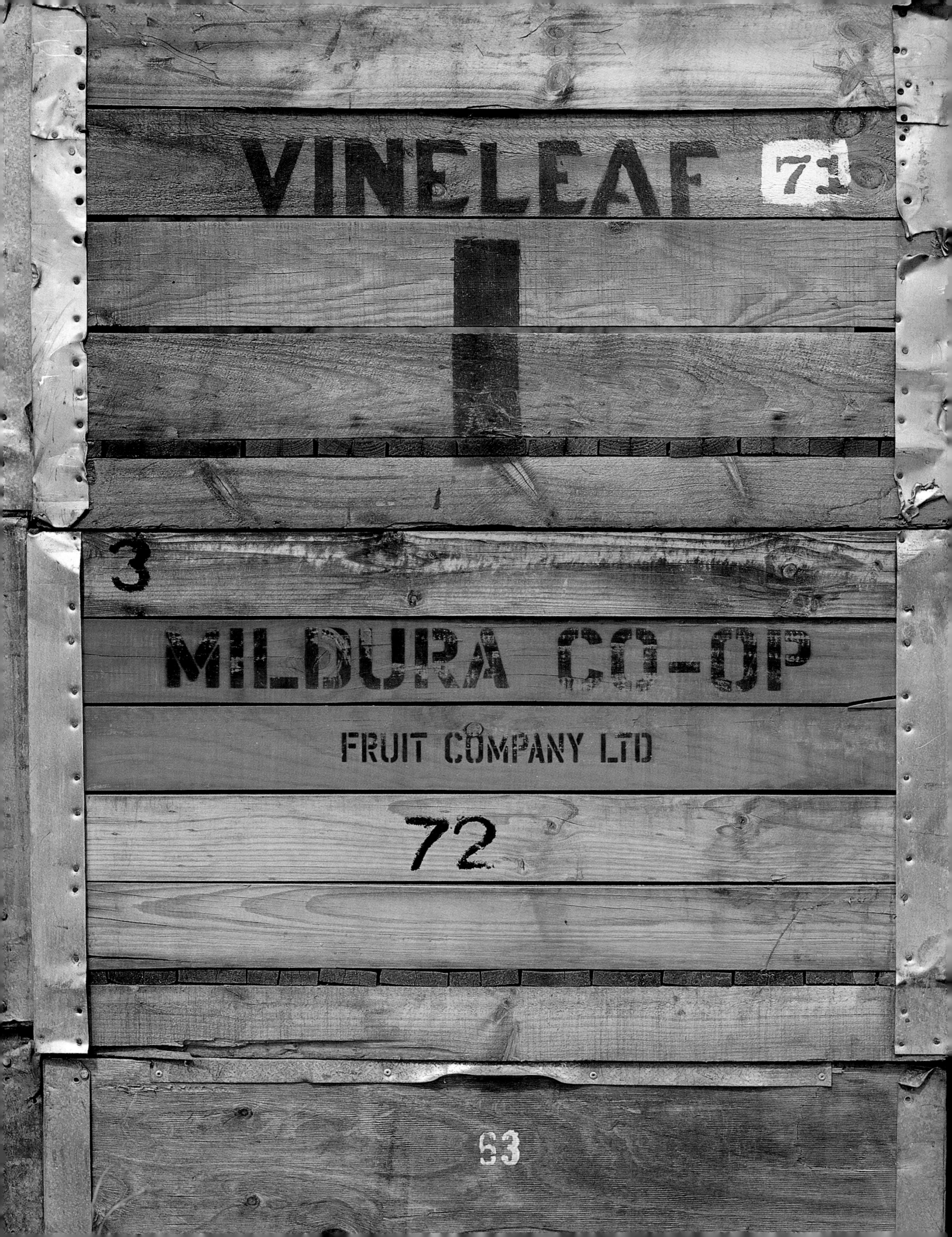

VINELEAF
71
3
MILDURA CO-OP
FRUIT COMPANY LTD
72
63

Modern Italian Food is a book of recipes for the home

cook. To my mind, there is very little of interest here to chefs, although some general directions are perhaps of some use to young industry people whose idea of Italian food has not yet been bastardised. My intention with this book is to reaffirm, time and again, the basic principles of Italian gastronomy: freshness, simplicity and lack of pretension. My friends say that when Italian food wants to get out of itself, it tries to become French – and I agree with that assessment. It is not right for Italian food to deviate from what it is. When it tries hard to be something else, it stops being Italian; it ceases to be fresh and simple.

introduction

This fresh and simple cuisine relies on a number of pillars: good olive oil, the judicious use of salt, fantastic cheese – Parmigiano Reggiano being the main one – golden chicken stock, home-made foods such as pasta, gnocchi and bread, the smart use of the lesser cuts of meat, the equally smart use of less glamorous fish and a love of texture over presentation.

I have divided the book into chapters devoted to a theme or ingredient, rather than going for the traditional division of entrée, main and dessert. The restrictions imposed by the meal divisions force food into a straitjacket, instead of allowing for greater freedom of choice at a communal table. Philosophically, besides food being good and wholesome, what is important for me is the communal aspect of the table. In an age when going fast is just about the only way, fitting in a restaurant or take-away meal here and there, the communal table in the privacy of one's home is the last refuge against insanity.

I have also included a chapter on wine. Not enough Italian cookery books deal with the wines of the peninsula, and look at creating a dialogue between food and wine. I think that the existing division between oenology and food is silly, as the two go together. Cooks and winemakers operate in the same field, yet rarely do they come together. What is important, in terms of this book, is that there are Italian wines that have now made Australia their home, with more doing so as time goes by. When you go out for dinner, it may happen that a sommelier suggests a glass of Soave or Sangiovese or Nebbiolo made, not in Italy, but in Australia. So, to a certain extent, this is a modern development, as the vinification of Shiraz is a modern development in Piedmont. Hence the title *Modern Italian Food,* which should read 'food, wine and all the other things that we are inventing or discovering as we go along in Australia'. 'Modern' also means that there is a definite trend in this book away from the over-use of tomato and garlic in favour of the smart use of olive oil as the saucing agent or flavouring, with herbs such as rosemary, sage, flat-leaf parsley and basil.

I have also blended sweet and savoury recipes under a general heading. So the chapter on flour contains bread, pasta and desserts, but then desserts also reappear under cheese, for obvious reasons.

Finally, there is a chapter on preserves and jams – a natural for me, as I live in an area that is rich in citrus and stone fruits and, like my friend Maggie Beer, I was taken by the rich possibilities of non-industrial conserves. Preserves and conserves are beautiful reflections of the gastronomic possibilities in farming communities. I hope that you will find a recipe or two that suits you.

Modern Italian Food is my third book in a short time. It feels somewhat odd to be a food writer because I never consciously aspired to be one: I became involved with food through necessity rather than choice. Now I find myself entangled in food as a professional, even though sometimes my inner self tells me that I should be doing something else. How many industries can boast such immediacy between the product and the consumer? And where each mouthful is not only a sensory experience open to immediate judgement, but also an immediate evaluation of its monetary worth? And where each newly trained employee is likely to move on, seeking a new professional experience? I choose to ignore that nagging voice from inside because food, for me, has now become a way of life and, more importantly, an excuse for trying out some ideas on an audience willing to listen. I was fortunate to have had a television series that provided me with a space to speak out about environmental issues, and to advance ideas that are important to me.

As usual, I have obtained permission from a few generous friends to reproduce their poems in this book. I thank them. I sincerely hope that you will enjoy this selection. That will be the best way to repay them for their generosity.

Hay Plain

O mirage
rolling wall of white
like of mirror
leakage of sky:
what pale sailors bloat
beneath your flooded trees?
We are almost upon the milk road,
drawing on scraps of scattered stars,
crow-coloured cows alongside,
a sea of snow
tumbling from the horizon

At sunset, pink haze beckons
To where the firebird blazes.

I like this poem by Kathleen Stewart, a
regular at the Mildura Writers' Festival,
because it is about the Hay Plain, an
important connection on the road to
Mildura for those approaching it from
the east.

sale

salt

'no salt, no flavour', my mother used to say. Not that she was driven to use salt to excess; she simply knew that salt brought out flavour when used appropriately and judiciously.

It seems to me most appropriate to begin *Modern Italian Food* with a chapter on salt. Salt is one of the oldest known preserving agents; salted meats and fish go back to the dawn of modern gastronomy. Salt-mining or harvesting and salt trading played as much a part in modern economic development as other minerals. The ability of the Venetians to harvest salt and to exchange it with their northern European neighbours for money or goods is well documented. Conversely, we know that in countries like England salt was so valued that it was stored in the same way as jewellery.

Modern medicine tells us that salt hardens the arteries and that this can damage our cardiovascular system. This is probably true in the same way that wine can be bad for you when it's consumed to excess. The combination of excessive salt consumption, a diet high in fast food and soft drink and a sedentary lifestyle do contribute to health problems. But this is not a problem with the salt itself: it is a dietary problem, most likely rooted in social causes.

My focus here is on 'good' salt, the carefully selected salt that we use to flavour or enhance a balanced and exciting diet.

To begin, the choice of salt is important: it is not simply a case of all salt being the same. The sources of salt can be very diverse – straight from the sea, from rocks or from ancient sea deposits. Each will have a small trace of different minerals, which provide for some flavour complexity. For example, in my part of the world in northern Victoria, locally harvested Mildura salt comes from ancient seawater deposits and is very flavoursome. Its high magnesium content gives it a pretty pink hue. When flaked, Mildura salt has a pleasant crunch, while its taste is regarded as 'sweeter' than most other salts.

Mildura salt – marketed as Murray River Salt – is also a good substitute for expensive imported salts, as is Horizon salt from Pyramid Hill, a little further north of Bendigo in Victoria. There is no need to buy Maldon sea salt imported from England (a country that could never make salt in the past), even though it might be interesting to have both at hand for comparison. Australia is the most salinity-affected country in the world and the thought of importing salt makes me cringe. However, in the interests of gastronomy, do have a look at French grey, wet sea salt or Sicilian sea salt, all of which are available from specialist stores.

In the area of north-west Victoria, around the Hattah and Pink Lakes, salt-mining goes back to the late nineteenth century. Afghani camel-drivers were known to have started an industry there, which relied on Murray River navigation for the transportation of the product to various inland ports.

As for me, whenever I dress a ripe red tomato with some Murray River flaky salt, I cannot help but think of the old days of paddle steamers and camels and let myself be carried away by a little bit of romance!

ocean trout in a salt crust
serves 8

In the endless quest for something different, many restaurants serve food that has been baked in a salt crust. I used to think that this was a kind of 'show off' practice, until I discovered that it's actually a very good method of cooking uniformly and evenly. A big fish, for instance, will cook evenly and keep very moist if baked in a salt crust. I cannot get the same result by poaching the fish in liquid. Whole salmon or ocean trout are the best fish to use with this method as they are naturally oily and moist. The salt seems to trap the moisture within the flesh – provided it is not overcooked.

Choose a fish weighing around 2 kg that will fit easily into a normal domestic oven. This will feed several people and any leftovers will keep for several days in the fridge and are lovely in salads or sandwiches.

Mayonnaise is the best condiment to serve with this fish and it is even better if you add a few salmon eggs or a little finely chopped garlic to the basic recipe. Do not use extra-virgin olive oil' for this mayonnaise – it is far too strongly flavoured.

10 egg whites
2 kg fine cooking salt
150 g cornflour
1 x 2 kg ocean trout
1 bunch flat-leaf parsley or
    a similar herb
mayonnaise
5 egg yolks
500 ml extra-light olive oil
1 teaspoon salt
3 teaspoons lemon juice, or more
    to taste
5 teaspoons salmon eggs (optional)
½ teaspoon finely chopped garlic
    (optional)

Preheat the oven to 200°C.
Beat the egg whites until stiff. Transfer to a large bowl and mix in the salt and flour, without overworking, until you obtain a mixture with a consistency a little like snow. Spread a third of this mixture on a baking tray, to a depth of about 1 cm. Place the fish on top and stuff the herbs into the fish cavity. Cover evenly with the remaining mixture. Bake for 25 minutes, then remove from the oven and leave to rest for a further 25 minutes.

Use a sharp knife to remove the crust, taking care not to damage the fish within. It should be perfectly cooked to pink. Do not worry if it is slightly undercooked close to the bone. Set that section aside and return it to the oven for a few more minutes.

To make the Mayonnaise, in a largish bowl beat the eggs yolks together and very gradually begin adding the oil bit by bit, until the mixture starts to emulsify. As the mixture thickens, add the salt and lemon juice. Beat in all the remaining oil (it could probably take even more) or until the mayonnaise reaches your desired consistency. Stir in the salmon eggs and garlic, if desired.

If the mayonnaise separates, start again with 2 fresh egg yolks, beating in the split mayonnaise bit by bit. Finally, add a little extra oil to bind it together, as you will now have used a total of 7 yolks.

Accompaniment: This dish is best served with a medley of grilled vegetables or some simple steamed potatoes and vegetables. If grilling, cut zucchini, eggplant and capsicum into manageable strips, brush with olive oil and grill, turning constantly, until golden brown.

Alternatively, place the vegetable strips on a tray lined with baking paper. Brush with olive oil and bake in a preheated 200°C oven for 20–25 minutes, or until cooked. Prepare each vegetable separately as they each need a different cooking time.

salmon cured with honey and salt
serves 6 or more

A strange combination indeed, but the contrast between the salt and honey makes the fish appealingly sweet and sour. I am rather keen on Mildura flaked salt – or Murray River salt – and the wonderful honey which derives mostly from the citrus groves of Sunraysia produced by my neighbours, the Monson family. If you notice some insistence on salmon in my recipes, it is because it is a readily available and versatile fish.

1 x 1 kg (or less) side of salmon, pin
  bones removed
1 cup citrus or other honey
1 cup flaked salt
1 tablespoon crushed coriander seeds
1 bunch coriander leaves, roughly
  chopped

Place the fish on a tray that will fit in your fridge. Spread the honey all over the salmon. Stir together the salt, coriander seeds and leaves and smear this mixture all over the salmon. Cover the fish with clingfilm and refrigerate for 24 hours. From time to time you can baste the fish with any juices that run off.
To serve, drain off the marinade and reserve. Slice the salmon thinly and serve drizzled with a little of the marinade and thin slices of toast.
If you like, serve the cured salmon with a frisée lettuce salad and a simple dressing made from lemon juice, olive oil and a little salt.

spaghetti with bottarga
serves 4

Bottarga is the salted, pressed and dried roe (fish eggs) of either the tuna or gray mullet and is a specialty of both Sardinia and Sicily. It has a pungent, sharp and salty flavour – a bit like a fishy sort of prosciutto – and yet is strangely delicate. While I usually try to avoid recipes with hard-to-find ingredients, I make a few exceptions if I think the result is worth the effort. Tuna bottarga is reasonably easy to find, and I understand that it is even being produced in Queensland. Anyway, the recipe is simplicity itself – it's almost too easy!

400 g spaghetti
4 tablespoons extra-virgin olive oil
100 g bottarga, finely shaved
4 tomatoes, peeled and chopped

Cook the spaghetti in plenty of salted boiling water until *al dente*, then drain well. Toss with the olive oil, bottarga and tomatoes, and serve.

roasted capsicum with anchovy cream
serves 6 as antipasto

Red and yellow capsicum are, to me, one of the most beautiful sights in nature. When roasted on an open flame, their charred skins emanate a special, unique and inviting smell. Large pieces of roasted capsicum, drenched in olive oil, anchovies, garlic and flat-leaf parsley make a meal that will never go out of fashion. Add a few good olives, some capers, a few thin slices of prosciutto, best quality mozzarella and some properly baked crusty bread for one of the easiest lunches on earth.

3 thick-fleshed red capsicum
3 thick-fleshed yellow capsicum
  (or use another 3 red capsicum)
1 clove garlic, peeled
100 ml extra-virgin olive oil
12 best-quality anchovy fillets
a few sprigs of fresh flat-leaf parsley
  or basil leaves

On the open flame of a gas stove, char the capsicum until you see the skin blackening and starting to peel. You can also achieve this on the grill of the barbecue. When the skins are black all over, remove the capsicum from the flame and cool. Peel and discard the blackened skin, and use kitchen paper to wipe the flesh clean – it's best to avoid rinsing them under water. Split the capsicum in half, remove and discard all the seeds and membrane. Place the flesh in a large flat serving dish.
Put the garlic in a food processor with a little of the oil and pulse until finely chopped. Add the anchovies and a little more oil and pulse to a cream. Add extra oil if needed. Pour the cream over the capsicum. Tear the parsley or basil leaves and scatter over the top before serving. Add extra oil if desired.

10 eggs

900 g plain flour

200 g fine cooking salt

1 x 1.7 kg best-quality
    free-range chicken

stuffing

2 tablespoons butter

2 tablespoons extra-virgin olive oil

200 g assorted exotic mushrooms,
    such as enoki or oyster mushrooms

200 g chicken livers, cleaned, left whole
    and marinated in Marsala for a few hours

1 clove garlic, finely chopped

salt and pepper

5 sage leaves

sauce

100 g porcini mushrooms

300 ml cream

1 tablespoon butter

1 tablespoon finely chopped flat-leaf parsley

Just try it! This is no ordinary way of cooking chicken. Rather, the bird is baked and steamed at the same time, because the crust keeps all the moisture inside.

What follows is a basic recipe, my adaptation of a wonderful dish I have eaten at Cheong Liew's restaurant, The Grange, in Adelaide. The chicken was stuffed with a mixture of its livers and exotic mushrooms, then enveloped in a crust and cooked to perfection. The presentation was spectacular. My guess is that, towards the end of the cooking time, pieces of puff pastry were attached to the sides of the chicken crust. These were removed at the table and set aside while the crust was ceremoniously 'broken'. The chicken was then carved and served to each diner with a piece of puff pastry, some of the stuffing and a rich poultry gravy. Many Chinese restaurants offer a dish called Beggar's Chicken, which is cooked in a similar way, but in clay. You can 'Italianise' this dish by preparing a sauce made of porcini mushrooms and a little cream to serve with the chicken. Or you can do away with the cream altogether, replacing it with a concentrated chicken stock.

chicken in a salt and flour crust | serves 4–6

To make the Crust, place the eggs, flour and salt in a large bowl and mix to form a smooth, malleable dough, adding a little water if necessary. The dough is quite stiff.

To make the Stuffing, heat the butter and oil in a large non-stick pan. Cook the mushrooms and livers until they are just seared to a light golden brown. Stir in the garlic and season with salt and pepper. Tear the sage and scatter over the mixture. Remove the pan from the heat and leave to cool.

When ready to cook, preheat the oven to 200°C. Line a baking tray with greaseproof paper or aluminium foil.

Wipe and dry the chicken inside and out, and fill the cavity with the stuffing.

Divide the dough in half and on a clean, floured work surface, roll out each piece to a thickness of a little under 1 cm. Place a piece of dough on the baking tray, and put the chicken on top, breast side up. Cover with the second piece of dough, pressing the edges together so that the bird is completely covered and sealed (use a little water if necessary). Bake at 200°C for 10 minutes, then lower the temperature to 180°C and cook for a further hour. Remove the bird from the oven and leave to rest for 20 minutes before serving. The chicken can rest for up to an hour in its crust and still retain its heat. These cooking instructions serve as a basic guideline; depending on your oven, the thickness of your dough and the quality of the chicken, there may be some variation.

To make the Sauce, soak the mushrooms in twice their volume of warm water for about 10 minutes to reconstitute. Place the cream in a saucepan and simmer until reduced by half. Squeeze the mushrooms dry, discarding the soaking water. Heat the butter in a small pan, then add the mushrooms and sauté for a few minutes until warmed through. Add the cream and simmer for a few more minutes. Season with salt and pepper and, just before serving, stir in the parsley. A nice alternative to the mushroom sauce is a reduced tarragon cream sauce. Simply add 1 tablespoon finely chopped French tarragon and 1 tablespoon finely chopped parsley to the reduced cream and season with salt and pepper. Pour the cream sauce over the chicken to serve.

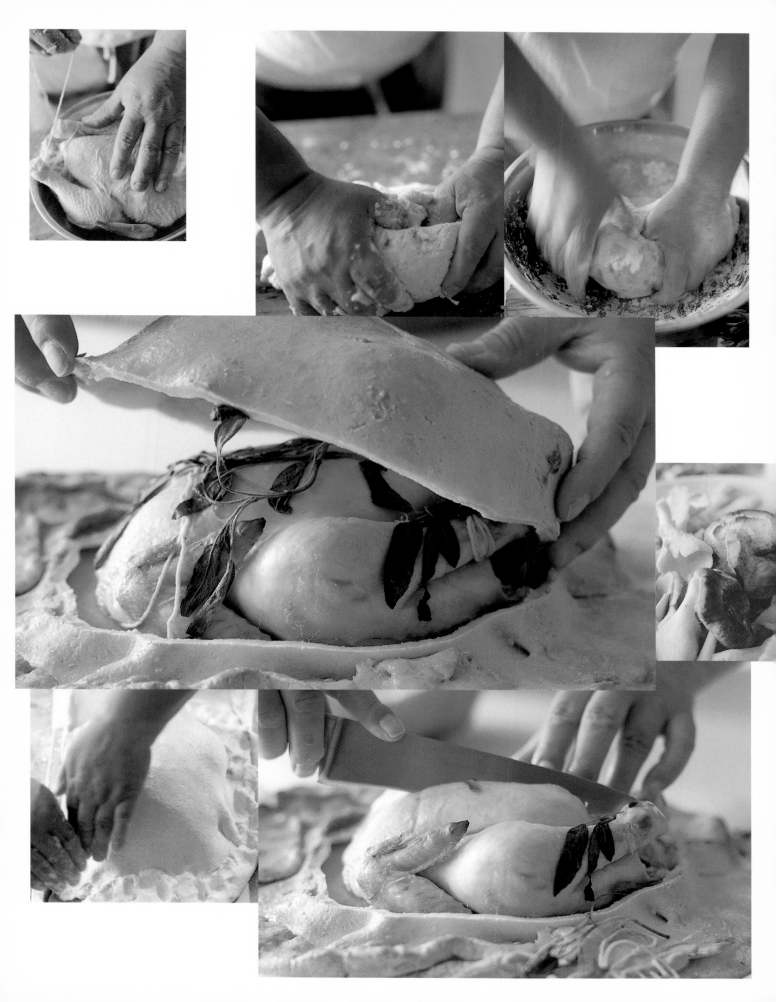

water If you are interested in food, I hope you are also interested in where it is grown, how and by what methods. Inevitably, you will have to look at how it is manufactured or transformed, transported and delivered – and by whom, and at what price.

These are all exquisitely political issues. Unfortunately, as food becomes entangled in fads and fashion in a more and more complex economy, we lose sight of where it comes from. Australians, who live mostly in the big coastal cities of our continent, have only vague ideas about where and how food is grown. Many are unaware of the nexus between food and water; in my darkest moments, I imagine most of the population of Australia mentally drifting away from the physical reality of the land they live on.

We must revere our waterways as they are the primary source of our food; equally, we must relinquish all unnecessary activities that are detrimental to the long-term wellbeing of the rivers, the environment they support, and the communities that depend on them.

To achieve this, green politics should be as much a part of each political party's language as are welfare and education. Green politics is not a middle-class luxury any more – if it ever was. It is a must for each and every farmer, and each and every city dweller. Green is not a dirty word. The removal of most trees to make room for pastures and farming has done enormous damage to the soil. As water falls from the sky – or irrigation, for that matter – and isn't absorbed by trees, it makes the salty water table rise. The vast Mallee country in north-west Victoria is a typical example of the slash-and-burn approach to land use. Geologists know that under the Mallee there is a huge water table with salt at five times greater than that found at sea level. The removal of trees allows rainwater to top up this vast bubble of underground water, which, as it expands, in geological time, will need to escape somewhere, possibly into the Murray River. Should it matter to us whether or not rivers live or die? It should, especially if it can be shown that its death is caused by humans rather than the cycle of nature. It should, because it is the integral part of a complex river system that defines much of the character of Australia itself.

The natural environment is the site of the spiritual connection between people and nature. We have celebrated enough the deeds of the white settlers, their sacrifices and achievements in opening up the outback. It is now time to consider, in the light of contemporary knowledge, how the disasters caused by the age of optimism can be contained.

Salting cod – when the fish is preserved in salt – is one of the most ancient methods of food preserving. Sadly, the Atlantic and North Sea cod that are so loved by the southern Mediterranean countries have been depleted by centuries of over-fishing. These days cod is virtually a protected species and what is sold as salt cod in many Italian delis is in fact ling, which is another fish altogether.

Some might argue that salt preserving is a time-consuming method of food preserving, that modern advances in refrigeration and freezing have made the practice obsolete.

The thing is, salt-preserved cod is truly one of the great flavours of the world, which should be retained at all costs; its unique texture cannot be matched.

To prepare, place salted cod in a bowl of water to soak. Change the water a few times until the salt is removed.

500 g salted cod, soaked

1 litre milk

2 litres water

5 peppercorns

1 bay leaf

100 ml light olive oil

1 clove garlic, finely chopped

baccalà mantecato | creamed cod | serves 6

Place the cod in a large pan with the milk, water, peppercorns and bay leaf. Bring to a boil, then lower the heat and simmer for about 10 minutes. The cod should be fairly soft to the touch. Turn off the heat and leave the fish to cool in the liquid. Strain through a sieve, discarding the liquid.

Remove and discard any bones (keep the skin), flake the fish and place in an electric mixer with the skin.

Using a paddle beater attachment, slowly beat the fish while gradually adding the olive oil and garlic.

The paddle beats the oil into the fish rather than breaking it down to a gluey paste as a food processor would do.

Refrigerate until ready to serve.

Serve on grilled or toasted rustic bread as an appetiser.

baccalà When I am mildly upset with my children, I call them *baccalà*. That translates roughly into something like 'duffer' or 'dill' or the more colourful 'dag'. Baccalà is salted cod, or *morue* if you go French. I was happy to learn from the authoritative book by Mark Kurlansky, *Cod: A biography of the fish that changed the world*, that the Danish word for cod, *torsk*, also has the colloquial meaning 'fool' and that in nineteenth-century England cod meant 'a joke or prank'.

I recommend *Cod* to all who are interested in the history of food. It documents the role that cod had in the economy of northern Europe and North America; it shows its influence over the cuisine of many countries; it highlights how culture in general can be shaped by a single ingredient; and it focuses on the tragic fact that the most important fish in history is facing extinction.

Australians are not passionate about cod, probably because we are geographically removed from the cod's sphere of influence. Yet I thought that there was enough of Britain's influence over early Australia to support a mild interest in salted or dried cod. The fish preserves well, and if it preserves well it can travel well, which may have helped in the old days.

It may be that, unfortunately, to desalinate a cod or to tenderise a dry one, far too much water is required, and Australia is not water-rich. Many European farm-houses or city squares have the advantage of fountains pouring water continuously.

I often tell my children about the so-called 'baccalà run' I enjoyed every Friday on my way to school. The stink emanating from the tub of cod outside the fishmonger's shop was so strong we'd block our noses and run past it screaming in unison. The 'baccalà run' became such a ritual it was not unusual to see thirty or so kids running past the fish shop screaming and laughing hysterically.

Salted or dried cod is not hard to find in Australia now, mainly because all the Latino races and the Greeks like it a lot. The most precious air-dried cod is a variety called Ragno, which I have found at the Mediterranean Supermarket in Melbourne, a favourite food haunt.

One of the problems with dried baccalà is that you need to bash it with a mallet before softening it in water for up to five days – and I suggest using the garage during the winter months if you wish to experiment. Baccalà dealers overseas have tenderising equipment and sell baccalà ready to go, if not outright cooked in two or three styles.

Salted baccalà is a lot easier to handle and only takes about 24 hours to desalinate with frequent changes of water. It is versatile, once reconstituted, because it can be fried, baked, cooked with tomato as a casserole, or boiled and used in a salad.

sardines preserved in salt

You can find salted sardines in great, big, colourful tins in some delis in the central markets of Australian cities. I think they truly are the caviar of the sea, the ultimate delicacy, and a great versatile food enhancer. Admittedly they are a little fiddly. They need to be rinsed of excess salt and deboned, and the scales need to be removed. Open up the sardines with your hands, and pull away the bones. Discard the tails and rinse the fish well to get rid of the scales and excess salt. Pat dry with kitchen paper.

Mix the fillets with butter in a food processor for the best condiment to serve with a barbecued steak or a simple sauce for quick spaghetti. Another way of using them is to melt them down in a mixture of butter and olive oil, which you then add to finely sliced and braised onions – and I mean braised to meltdown point. Pour the mixture on home-made spaghetti and sprinkle liberally with cheese – you can't go wrong! I know that many diners are a little indifferent to this type of preserved fish – they even refer to anchovies as the 'hairy things' and carefully avoid them in Caesar salad. But for once, try them.

sardine butter for steaks
makes enough for 4 steaks

100 g butter at room temperature
4 sardines, scaled and deboned
  and rinsed of salt

Place butter and sardines in a food processor and blend. Or, place in a bowl and work in the fillets and butter until a paste is achieved.

sardine sauce with onions
serves 4

2 tablespoons butter
2 tablespoons extra-virgin olive oil
4 large brown onions, finely sliced
4 cloves garlic, finely chopped
8 salted sardines, filleted and washed
salt and pepper, to taste
400 g spaghetti
4 tablespoons coarsely chopped
  flat-leaf parsley
freshly grated Grana Padano cheese,
  to taste

Melt the butter and olive oil in a pan and slowly cook the onions and garlic until very soft. You may need to add water or more olive oil as you go. When the mixture is very soft and a light golden brown, stir in the sardines. Season with salt and pepper to taste.

Cook the spaghetti in plenty of boiling salted water until *al dente* and drain well. Add the sauce and toss well. Serve with a sprinkling of parsley and cheese to taste.

The anti-salt phobia, coupled with a general lack of knowledge about Italian cooking, means that all too often pasta is cooked in unsalted water. This drives me nuts! It is particularly maddening when one has to explain to new apprentices in the restaurant kitchen who do not take the instruction seriously.

I can only imagine the training schools and colleges do not reinforce the practice.

So, here are the principles for cooking pasta: first, the water must be salted so that it tastes almost like sea water. That means using at least one tablespoon of salt per litre of water.

Second, commercial pasta must be cooked *al dente*, not just for taste and texture, but also for health reasons. If you read your Atkins diet book, you will discover that the complex carbohydrates in pasta are more easily absorbed by the body if the pasta is cooked soft. If you cook your spaghetti *al dente*, then – Atkins says – almost 20 per cent of the carbohydrates will pass through you instead of into you!

Third, if you work in commercial kitchens and need to pre-cook your pasta, pre-cook it very *al dente*. Do not plunge it into cold water, but spread it out on your work bench to cool. Drizzle it with a little oil to prevent sticking. When needed, plunge the pasta into hot, salted water and cook for as little as 20 seconds. This will ensure that it stays fresh and *al dente*. And there is no reason for adding oil to the cooking water.

home-made spaghetti | serves 4

Here is a traditional pasta recipe that uses 3 large (61 g) eggs and 300 g flour. There are various kinds of pasta flour available in Italian delis, but normal plain flour will do just as well if you can't locate pasta flour. Do not add any salt to the dough; the salt will be in the water when you cook the pasta. To make, just mix the paste by hand until you have a smooth shiny dough that is neither wet nor dry. Rest for a while and then roll out the dough using a pasta machine. The settings usually go from 1 to 8 or 9. I suggest you start with 1 and make a nice, even sheet by folding in on itself and rolling through the machine a few times.

Change to setting 3 and roll it through a few more times. Finally, roll it through a couple of times on a 6 or 7 setting. Cut the large piece into smaller pieces about 25 cm long and run them through the spaghetti cutter. They'll come out nice and thick. Cook the pasta straight away or freeze it (I like to spread it out in pizza boxes). Cook the frozen pasta straight from the freezer. Obviously the cold will lower the water temperature, so make sure the water is boiling really vigorously.

These make a delightful addition to an antipasto selection and are delicious served as a salty/hot accompaniment to poached meats like cotechino. Readily available long red chillies are ideal: they are hot, but not mouth-blisteringly so.

10 red chillies
500 ml olive oil
20 best-quality anchovies
1 teaspoon small capers per chilli

peperoncini ripieni di capperi e acciughe | chillies stuffed with anchovies | makes 10

Use a sharp knife to slit the chillies lengthwise and remove the seeds (you may want to wear gloves). Heat the oil, but not to smoking point. Drop in the chillies and let them steep in the oil for a few minutes. Take care not to overcook or the skins will come off and they will look wrinkly and unappetising.
Remove the chillies from the oil and drain on kitchen paper.
Chop the anchovies and mix with the capers. When the chillies are cool enough to handle, fill each with the anchovy mixture. Serve with any boiled meats or as part of an antipasto platter.

pork I once saw a photograph in a pig farmers' magazine of a Belgian breed of pork 'assembled' some years ago for maximum meat content. It looked shocking. This animal had none of the familiar attributes of a piggy: a nice, friendly face, pinky complexion, curly tail and dainty trotters. Babe did not need to go to the city to get to see the dark side of things: all he had to do was to go to his nearest library to read what is happening to his relations all over the world – and here in Australia.

Had Babe seen what I had, he would have immediately touched his behind, to check if he too had a bum hanging out like some baboons in the zoo. Then he would have looked at himself and flexed his muscles to detect any sign of becoming like a body builder on steroids.

The pig in question could only move, I'd imagine, like a body builder gone silly. Its muscle looked like such that its movements – if allowed – would have to be short and jerky movements, with none of that trotting pace of healthy pigs roaming around in the open. Nothing like the proverbial pig of St Anthony, the pig that moved about freely in the old Italian village, fed by everyone and given to the priest as a form of payment when nice and fat.

There is no fat in modern pigs. No one wants to know about fat any more. It is bad for you, they say. The more meat on a pig, the more profit, because there is no use for fat. Pigs are now bred for meat only, at the expense of flavour. Whether you like it or not, fat *is* flavour and, what's more, you do not have to eat it if you do not want to. You can leave it on the plate, or you can eat it sparingly, but pork without fat is tasteless.

Not only that, the genetic pool is being restricted by favouring only certain types of pig: those that put on 2 kg a day, those that conform to the market necessity of the most meat, achieved as quickly as possible to be sold competitively and with a margin on it.

What I worry about is the disappearance of animals that taste better and would taste even better if fed properly. To maintain demand, there has to be some need and I suppose that would not be too difficult to achieve. Consumers have to be prepared to pay a little bit more and not to allow themselves to be brain-washed about fat.

I stand in supermarket queues and perv into people's shopping trolleys. It is a sport I enjoy. I do not mind waiting for 20 minutes or more. Defamation laws prevent me from writing what I think about what I see. Some products would certainly cause obesity and cardiovascular problems, but none has received the attention that pork has, or has been transformed to the same extent in the name of health.

It is very hard for professional cooks to deal with pork, let alone modern pork. In the past there was a bit of a fad for pork fillet covered with dried fruit sauces, but mercifully, that soon died. Asian restaurants, particularly the Chinese ones, use more pork on average, because in their tradition they have wonderful recipes and amazing skills at transforming the meat – think about those delicious little morsels at *yum cha*. Pork is found in some modern Australian restaurants in the guise of the Italian sausage cotechino, but as a dish, roast pork, for instance, is only found in bistros catering for a diminishing clientele.

There are few producers out there who do exceptional things, but they tend not to be too well known. Some do not even want to be known at all, because they cannot gear up for a significant production in a very adverse market situation.

These matters are complex and they reflect, once again, the contradiction of mass production with the wishes of the cook. Other countries address the problem differently, so there are models out there for better pork produce.

The latest research shows that pork fat has much less cholesterol than butter, fewer calories than olive oil and is a good source of protein. Italians have known this for a long time, but it seems that the Americans have just discovered this. So they are finally tasting, in up-market restaurants, thinly sliced pork lard – the very same snack that I enjoyed after school, before the daily soccer encounters with my mates!

salt preserves anything, and smallgoods such as salame and prosciutto would not exist without salt. Nor would sausages. Minced pork, mixed with a little salt and black pepper, is the basis of the so-called continental sausages, such as the famous ones made by my friend and fellow Trevisano, Gianni Gianfreda (known as Jonathan), proprietor of Jonathan's butcher shop in Melbourne.

Pork mince cured in the same way as for salame is the base for many pasta sauces, risotto (in the winter), frittata or for stuffing. Instead of stuffing the mince into the gut casings – as with traditional salame or sausages – you can simply mix the meat with salt and pepper, roll it into a sausage shape, wrap it in clingfilm and store it in the fridge.

The mixture will not keep very long (perhaps a week) but you can use it in so many different ways. It is particularly good as a sauce for fettuccine, made into a tomato or cream sauce, and it makes a deliciously hearty winter soup.

Select the best pork available, preferably from the shoulder, where there is a natural mixture of lean meat and fat. Get your butcher to mince the meat coarsely, and make sure the animal was a female (sow). Male pigs are not castrated in Australia so their meat has a strong urine smell and flavour.

salame meat with one hundred uses
makes 5 x 200 g portions

1 clove garlic, roughly chopped
25 ml red wine
1 kg pork mince
15 g salt
3 g coarsely ground black pepper
a pinch of freshly grated nutmeg
a pinch of ground cinnamon

Put the garlic and wine into a glass and leave to infuse for 2 hours. Pour through a fine strainer, reserving only the wine.

Place the remaining ingredients in a large bowl and use your hands to mix together thoroughly. Add the garlic-infused wine and mix again. Divide the mixture into 5 portions and roll each out to a small sausage shape. Wrap in clingfilm like a small salami and refrigerate until needed.

salame sauce
serves 4

Use as a sauce for Strozzapreti Pasta (see page 69).

1 tablespoon butter
1 tablespoon olive oil
1 onion, peeled and finely chopped
1 carrot, peeled and finely chopped
1 x 200 g portion of Salame (see
    this page)
50 ml white wine
100 g porcini mushrooms or normal
    cultivated mushrooms
100 ml cream
400 g Strozzapreti Pasta (see
    page 69)
fresh flat-leaf parsley
100 g parmesan, freshly grated

Heat the butter and olive oil in a pan and fry the onion and carrot until golden. Add the salame, stir in well and fry until it starts to colour. Add the wine and cook until it evaporates. Add the mushrooms, and cook for a few minutes. Then add the cream, lower the heat and simmer very gently for about 20 minutes.

To serve, cook the strozzapreti in plenty of boiling salted water until al dente. Drain well. Add the sauce and toss well. Serve with a sprinkling of parsley and parmesan to taste.

40 g butter

1 tablespoon extra-virgin olive oil

1 stick celery, finely chopped

1 onion, finely chopped

300 g Savoy cabbage, finely sliced

1 x 200 g portion of Salame (see page 23)

1.5 litres boiling Golden Chicken Stock (see page 79)

260 g Italian rice, preferably Vialone Nano

freshly grated parmesan (optional)

rice soup with salame and cabbage | serves 4

Melt the butter and oil in a large heavy-based pan set over a medium heat. As they sizzle, add the celery and onion. Stir for a few minutes, then add the cabbage and cook for a few more minutes. Add the salame and use a wooden spoon to stir it in well and break down any lumps.

After a few minutes, add the boiling broth and cook for 35–40 minutes. Add the rice, and cook for a further 10 minutes until the rice is cooked. Stir from time to time. Serve at once; cheese is optional.

olio di oliva

olive oil

nothing in the

food industry has stirred up passions – and moved dollars around – like the recent and burgeoning olive oil industry in Australia. Back in 1996 I was making my own first experiments in olive oil production out of a few trees on the Sturt Highway, in Buronga, NSW, with my mate Gianni Grigoletto, an industrial chemist who was struck by the olive oil-making fever. Since then millions of trees have gone into the ground from Queensland to Tasmania, from Victoria to Western Australia.

Australians are slowly taking to olive oil, perhaps not as quickly as hoped, but they are converting. As oil prices come down due to increased production, oil becomes slightly more affordable. Picking, crushing, transporting, bottling and labelling, storing and transporting again all conspire to keep the price of oil high. Most Australians tend to shop in supermarkets, and it is mighty hard to get good oil into price-driven outlets. The future for olive oil is still in the hands of passionate, small producers striving for quality. All we need is to persuade consumers – or a section of them – that olive oil is as worthy of immediate consumption as a bottle of Shiraz. There are many people who knock over a $30 bottle of wine in a matter of minutes. A bottle of oil, at the same price, is capable of producing greater gastronomic pleasure, but it is looked upon as a luxury.

My olive oil journey began somewhere in Balranald, lower NSW, about 180 kilometres from Mildura, a few years ago. Determined to have my own label, I bought the contents of two groves established by Sicilian migrants in the 1950s. Little did I know that I needed equipment to harvest, bins, a fork lift, a truck and, above all, a team of fast pickers. Bruce and Jenny Chalmers came into my life, in the way that angels do: they provided a team of fast (mostly) Cambodian pickers, the truck, the bins, the fork lift and the cash flow.

Determined to keep my family out of this ordeal (they thought I was a little crazy to be involved in an industry that we did not understand), I went off on a chilly May morning on my motorcycle, thinking I'd get to Balranald in a flash. I underestimated the coldness of the Australian morning: at Robinvale, 60 kilometres down the road, I began feeling the effects of hypothermia and halfway between Robinvale and Balranald, took off my undies and wrapped them around my neck to stop myself from freezing. Fourteen days of picking ensued, and I was oil rich in a few weeks. I completed my crazy and irrational project by purchasing a container of bottles from Italy, I was kept in oil for a long time. Somewhere, sometime during that period I met Peter Caird, oil-maker of Victorian Olive Groves (VOG). Besides Peter and his partner, VOG consisted of two more families, the Harts and the Zitos. Soon a partnership was formed between all of us and now VOG, with its proud label, and gold medal earned in Italy against 700 competitors, is proudly sold in many outlets, including David Jones and Harvey Nichols in London. From undies around the neck to David Jones – that's my idea of fun!

types of oil

Many consumers, even those who are keen olive oil consumers, are confused about the names of the olive varieties that appear on labels. The question I am asked all the time is, which oil is best? There is no short answer. We have over 100 varieties planted in Australia, some dating back to the 1800s. Various trials were made and varieties such as Manzanillo, Verdale and Barouni were planted with great enthusiasm even as recently as ten years ago, before people realised that perhaps they were not the right varieties for our conditions. Growers are a little more knowledgeable today, and what follows is the current commonly shared wisdom – the most succinct overview, a rough guide to understanding some of the names that appear on olive oil labels.

manzanillo

Originally a Spanish varietal and not used much for oil in Spain. In Australia Manzanillo probably represents more than 30 per cent of all plantings. It is a tricky fruit to process, but is capable of producing top-quality oils that are initially quite unbalanced. It would appear that this oil actually benefits from short-term rest before consumption, something that usually is not done. Manzanillo is high in bitterness and has a peppery finish. The bitterness is often much reduced when the oil comes into contact with food.

verdale

May be of French origin and produces one of the best oils in terms of taste and nose. The variety was planted extensively simply because it was available. The oil smells of fresh green grass and displays a light pungency. It is still my favourite oil to use when fresh. Unfortunately it does not produce much oil – producers are lucky to get 10 litres of oil, sometimes less, from 100 kg of olives. So Verdale has been relegated to the back burner, with literally thousands of trees here and there not harvested because of their low yields.

nevadillo blanco
This Spanish variety makes good oil in warmer climates. Nutty and grassy, with a great bite at the end.

picual
Another Spanish variety, and a newcomer. The only tastings I have seen come from trees that are not much more than three years old. It is nutty on the palate with pleasant aromas. It promises to do well, especially as it seems to yield 24 per cent oil, a vast improvement on other varieties.

arbequina
Also Spanish, and one of the mainstays of the Spanish oil industry. It looks promising, but Australian plantings are only very recent, so it is too early to tell.

sevillano
Another Spanish variety that is much better for preserving than for oil. It displays an odd palate and does not look like it is destined for greatness.

frantoio/corregiola/paragon
They are really close relatives. Frantoio is very much Tuscan. These all perform well in southern Australia and yield at least 25 per cent oil, with immediate balance of nose, aroma and taste. Big and bold, and also good for pickling.

leccino
Another Italian. The omens are great. Produces lots of oil with a distinctive character, but once again, it is too early to say.

barnea
An Israeli cultivar destined to become a favourite for the blenders of oil. It is a smooth oil without rough edges.

imported versus Australian My suggestion is simple. If you use a lot of oil, by all means buy the imported in the 3 or 4-litre cans. But for all your raw use of oil – to finish a dish, to dress a salad or boiled veggies, to complete mash potatoes, to liven up a soup, to drench bruschetta, to drizzle over grilled fish – use a fresh Australian oil.

Brian and Lynne Chatterton, respectively former Minister for Agriculture and agriculture adviser under the Dunstan government of South Australia, who now live in Umbria in Central Italy, put out a very interesting and personal book titled *Discovering Oil*. It is a great read on their personal olive oil journey. On the market for oil, they write: 'St Francis gave Umbria its title of "land of saints", but the Tuscans perform the miracle of the olive oil every day. The 300,000 tonnes of imported oil is simply made to disappear. We have never seen a bottle of olive oil in Italy or in NZ or Australia that has been labelled "Blend of Italian and Tunisian or Spanish olive oil", yet that must be the case. Tuscany exports more oil that it produces'.

So, if you can help the Australian producers, do so. At least many of us are contactable; we have websites and phone numbers. We are happy to get feedback, comments and suggestions. Together we can build a small and lively industry to be proud of.

Top Australian olive oils cost the same as the top olive oils of Europe. That is not to say that they are equal to the best in the world. The production costs are the same at the boutique end, so it is not like the Aussies are trying to rip you off.

Just remember that ours is a very young industry. There is so much to discover still, and many mistakes to be made yet.

pinzimonio

Here's a word to practise your Italian. Picture a selection of the freshest vegetables – fennel, capsicum, carrots, beans, celery hearts and whatever else you can think of – cut into sticks or bite-sized pieces, a bowl of the freshest, new season olive oil and a little Murray River salt. Dip the vegetables into the oil, dress with a bit of salt, and crunch. That is pinzimonio, one of the most astute ways of enjoying oil and stimulating the appetite.

During the 2004 Melbourne Wine and Food Festival I had the pleasure of eating some roasted piglet expertly cooked by Pietro Porcu of the popular restaurant Da Noi. This was served at the restaurant Scusami on the balcony overlooking the Yarra River, a perfect setting for an al fresco dinner. And sure enough, Pietro served the piglet cold, on a bed of myrtle leaves with large bowls of pinzimonio. The combination of crisp skin and raw vegetables was a refreshing change from the usual rich sauces that accompany roasted meats.

Salmon on offer in Australia is farmed, so it is always easy to find. As well as being a great source of omega 3 acids, which are good for you, the fish is relatively inexpensive. Poaching salmon in olive oil may seem very extravagant, but if you use the appropriate cooking vessel – something long and narrow, like a loaf-shaped baking tin – the amount of oil needed is not much at all. Furthermore, you can reuse the oil for cooking other fish recipes. It stores well in a jar.

The idea is to cook the fish very, very slowly for a relatively short time. The only thing you have to do is keep a watchful eye on it to make sure the fish doesn't overcook. The oil should be at a fairly low temperature (50–60°C), which is cool enough for you to stick your finger into it (although you wouldn't want to keep it there for too long). After 5–6 minutes the fish should be cooked to a perfect pink. If too many white dots appear on the surface of the fish, the oil is too hot and the fish is starting to overcook.

So, why bother with all this? Because there is simply no better way of preserving the integrity of the fish flesh, and when it melts in your mouth, you will agree that it is very appealing.

salmon cooked in olive oil
serves 4–6

enough good quality olive oil to cover the fish
1 large salmon fillet, about 800 g, bones removed and trimmed, skin on, or 4–6 individual pieces, to achieve more or less the equivalent weight

Heat the oil to about 55°C over a low heat. The oil only needs to be hot enough to cook the fish – if you can stick your finger into the oil and leave it there for a few seconds without getting burnt, it is probably about right. (Obviously, you need to exercise some caution when attempting this!) Slip the fish into the oil and cook for 5 minutes, watching to ensure it doesn't overcook. Use a large spatula or 2 spoons to very carefully remove the fish from the oil. Do not allow it to break if you possibly can. Serve the salmon warm with a simple potato salad tossed with soft-boiled eggs (see this page) and mayonnaise (see page 4).

potato salad with soft-boiled eggs
serves 4

Potatoes tossed in extra-virgin olive oil are simple and delicious. There are many other equally tasty variations that use the simple olive oil dressing as a base. Try tossing the potatoes with lightly cooked green beans and small black olives; or a few anchovies or flakes of tuna – fresh or tinned work well. Another good option is to toss through some small sweet cherry tomatoes and thin slices of Spanish onion.

6 waxy potatoes (desirées are ideal)
extra-virgin olive oil
a squeeze of lemon juice
salt and pepper to taste
3 soft-boiled eggs
fresh flat-leaf parsley or spring onions, coarsely chopped

Boil the potatoes until tender, then peel and cut into cubes. While they are still warm, put the potatoes into a large mixing bowl and toss with the remaining ingredients.

Spaghetti simply dressed with olive oil, garlic, flat-leaf parsley and a scattering of chilli flakes has been around since the proverbial cocky was an egg. This brilliant dish has not made it to the Australian repertoire of Italian dishes because Australians tend to not venerate spaghetti – we regard it as just another pasta option among many, nothing more, nothing less.

And yet spaghetti is so much more, especially spaghetti cooked properly *al dente*. In one of my previous books, I waxed lyrical about properly cooked spaghetti with butter. Naturally, instead of butter, one can also use olive oil – cholesterol free – and that other herb, garlic. For those who are interested, spaghetti is also 'Atkins approved' in the second stage of this popular low carbohydrate diet. Spaghetti aglio olio is a great party dish. When we entertain in large numbers and some type of fodder is needed to soak up alcohol, spaghetti aglio olio fits the bill. The aroma of fried garlic and chilli takes over the house and creates a great food atmosphere. In Italy it is often called spaghetti di mezzanotte, or midnight spaghetti, precisely because the dish is perfect when the munchies hit late at night.

spaghetti aglio, olio, peperoncino
serves 5–6

500 g spaghetti
200 ml good quality virgin olive oil
5 cloves garlic, peeled and sliced
1 teaspoon chilli flakes, or
    more to taste
plenty of fresh flat-leaf parsley leaves,
    roughly chopped
freshly grated parmesan

Bring a large pot of water to the boil. Salt it with at least 1 tablespoon of salt per litre of water. Cook the spaghetti until *al dente*, drain well and tip into a large bowl.
Meanwhile, heat the oil in a large frying pan and fry the garlic until golden brown. Add the chilli flakes to taste and remove from the heat.
Add the hot oil and parsley to the spaghetti and toss well. If you like your pasta a little more moist, add more olive oil or reserve a few tablespoons of the cooking water to stir through. Serve with cheese on the side so people may help themselves.

raw beetroot salad

I love the vibrant colour of beetroot, and home-cooked beetroot makes a spectacular addition to a summer salad of fresh veggies drenched in olive oil. But when you feel like something a little different from the norm, try this delicious salad, which uses raw beetroot rather than cooked. It is tossed with a few sultanas or other suitable dried grapes.

Simply peel the beetroot and grate it on the large holes of your grater. (If you have an electric appliance with a grating attachment, then use it by all means. But you may find it takes longer to set up the appliance than doing it manually.) Add a few sultanas or other dried grapes, drizzle on a little olive oil, a squeeze of lemon juice, a splash of vinegar and a good grind of salt. Fresh mint leaves add another dimension to the dish.

summer vegetables in olive oil
serves 6

Any assortment of vegetables – carrots, broccoli, snowpeas, beans and beetroot – can be lightly boiled, refreshed and then dressed with oil and salt to make a delicious summer vegetable salad. You can serve them hot, but to my mind there is nothing like a cold platter of gorgeous vegetables resplendent in a glossy coating of oil – and maybe a little vinegar and lemon juice – for a hot summer evening.

The Flying Spring Onion

The flying spring onion
flew through the air
over to where
the tomatoes grew in rows
and he said to those
seed-filled creatures
My rooted days are done,
so while you sit here
sucking sun
I'll be away and gone,
to Greenland
where they eat no green
and I won't be seen
in a salad bowl with you,
stung by lemon,
greased with oil,
and nothing at all to do
except wait to be eaten.
With that he twirled
his green propellers
and rose above the rows
of red balls
who stared as he grew small
and disappeared.

Matthew Sweeny is an Irish poet who
lives in London. One night, I organised
a dinner party for him, Maggie Beer
and Stephanie Alexander, which turned
into a memorable disaster! This poem
reminds me of Matthew's humour.

I was initially rather reluctant to include this recipe, but when Cheong Liew cooked it at the Mildura Writers' Festival for the guest of honour, Clive James, it occurred to me that this recipe is a real foodie treat and I should include it.

It is not Italian, really, because Italians prefer to boil the octopus, slice it thinly and then dress it with olive oil and lemon juice. However, its intentions are deeply Mediterranean.

Three ingredients are important here: the octopus, the garlic and the olive oil. Some attention to detail is needed in the cooking, but not overwhelmingly so. Served as an antipasto, you only need small portions.

1 litre olive oil, or enough to cover the octopus
4 thick octopus tentacles
1 head of really healthy garlic, broken into cloves
20 small black olives (optional)
2 or more long red chillies

octopus poached in olive oil | serves 4

Heat the oil in a small, heavy-based pot until it is almost smoking. Use a pair of tongs to carefully lower each octopus tentacle into the oil. When seared, remove the tentacle from the oil and set aside. When all the tentacles have been seared (and it only takes a few moments) lower the garlic into the oil, and then the olives and chillies. Return the octopus tentacles to the oil and lower the heat to the lowest possible temperature. Cook for about 25 minutes, or until the octopus is tender. Be careful not to overcook, or the octopus will turn a little pasty.

Use a slotted spoon to remove the octopus, garlic and olives from the oil. Allow to cool, then slice each octopus tentacle to your desired thickness. Use the olives and garlic cloves as a garnish – the garlic is perfect for squeezing out of its skin.

Cheong Liew served this poached octopus with a salad of green leaves, avocado and soft-boiled eggs. I guess you could also poach the eggs to end up with a sort of octopus Caesar Salad. A few anchovies would certainly not go astray here. Dress with the Mayonnaise from page 4.

The leftover oil There will be a lot of precious olive oil left over. There is also quite a lot of octopus juice mixed in as well, so I suggest you use it to make a rich tomato sauce. When in season, use fresh tomatoes, otherwise tinned ones will do. The idea is to end up with a good balanced sauce that tastes a little of octopus and is dense enough to serve with pasta. If you can, use home-made fresh pasta, as it is more porous than the dried varieties and will therefore absorb a fair bit of liquid.

A recipe passed on to me by Lynne and Brian Chatterton. They use
fresh sultana grapes in their recipe. I appreciate that unless you live in
a wine-growing area it can be difficult to obtain fresh sultana grapes.
But they do appear in the markets in February and March every year.
Alternatively, use another sweet table grape variety with small berries.

2 large eggs
150 g caster sugar
4 tablespoons olive oil
60 g butter
5 tablespoons milk
200 g plain flour
1 teaspoon baking powder
grated zest of 1 lemon
grated zest of 1 orange
a good grating of nutmeg
2 cups fresh sultana grapes
a little demerara sugar
icing sugar

olive oil and sultana cake | makes 1 x 23 cm cake

Preheat the oven to 180°C and grease and line a 23 cm springform cake tin.
Beat the eggs and sugar until pale and thick. Add the oil, butter and milk and mix well.
In a separate bowl, sift together the flour and baking powder and stir in the citrus zests and nutmeg.
Tip the dry ingredients into the batter and stir to combine. Add just over half the sultana grapes to
the batter and mix in briefly.
Pour the batter into the prepared cake tin and bake for 15 minutes. Remove from the oven and
sprinkle on the remaining sultana grapes and the demerara sugar. Return to the oven and cook for
a further 40 minutes. When cooked, remove from the oven, allow to cool and dust with icing sugar.
Serve on a bed of grape leaves.

I regard this simple and delicious cake
as an ideal way to introduce kids to both
cake-making and olive oil.

7 eggs, separated
200 g caster sugar
100 ml extra-virgin olive oil
160 g self-raising flour
150 g drinking chocolate, sifted
110 ml warm water

olive oil cake | serves 10

Preheat the oven to 180°C and grease and line a 23 cm cake tin.
Beat the egg yolks with 160 g of the caster sugar until light and fluffy. With the beater on medium
speed add the olive oil, a little at a time, as if you were making a mayonnaise. Change to a low speed
and add the dry ingredients, beating until combined. Add the water.
In a separate bowl, whip the egg whites until thick and foamy. Add the remaining caster sugar and
beat gradually until the mixture forms stiff, glossy peaks.
Fold the whites gently but quickly into the chocolate mixture. When well combined, pour into the
prepared cake tin and bake for 1 hour or until a cake-tester or skewer inserted in the middle of
the cake comes out clean.

frumento

wheat

should you be bothered making bread? Most people claim they do not have time, and yet bread is so primordial I believe people should have a go at making it at least once or twice in their lifetime.

So much bread sold commercially these days is applied chemistry, made with loads of preservatives – substances that prevent mould, that keep it moist, that give it colour and so on. White sliced bread often contains sugar so that it colours when toasted. It toasts to cardboard, anyway. As you can gather, my feelings toward sliced bread are very strongly negative. I am even more annoyed by the fact that large manufacturers are centralising their bread production in the metropolitan centres and then shipping it to regional areas on trucks. Where there used to be bakeries and skilled bakers, there is now a convenience store with crappy bread. Even existing bakeries, by and large, have succumbed to the magic of the pre-mix bag. That is, a bag of flour containing all the elements that will make bread once you add water to it. The art of baking with flour, yeast, salt and water and shaping that into breads with different personalities is becoming a thing of the past.

Yes, there are some good bakeries here and there, but these are the last heroes, the true believers, that in time will be trashed. The large food retailers – people who, to be fair, have done so much for vegetable varieties – have let bread go. Vast aisles, canyons indeed, of 'white death' is almost all they have to offer. 'White death' is what old-style bakers call the new stuff. On top of that there is a new dietary craze which asserts that bread and wheat products are not good for you. Excluding people with a coeliac condition – which can indeed be very nasty – this new food fashion had cost the British bread industry a whopping 10 per cent drop in sales in early 2004. Bread, confined between the pole of dietary fashion and the pole of crap, is bound not to have a future in most modern countries. It may well become a thing of the past.

Mildura, like most of rural Australia, is surrounded by wheat and sheep country. We grow great wheat that we export to the world and yet right through the vast Mallee we eat lousy bread. There are few bakers, and most use pre-mixed flour. Rural Australia makes vanilla slices out of pre-made pastry and packet custard.

I am ashamed of these practices, and I'd pay an arm and a leg to see a reversal of this shameful state of affairs.

When I found Bill Mayne, who was happy to move to the country to bake for me, I offered him a job and built him a bakery. If there is one product that I have been consistently happy and proud of, it is Bill's everyday bread. The sight of the golden bread, straight out of the oven, first thing in the morning has sustained me emotionally for the last three years.

I am also proud of my friendship with John Calvert, the owner–operator with Bronwyn of Irrawarra Bread in the Victorian Western District. Affectionately known to me as Johnny Mutton, John always had a food dream. We met as young lads picking grapes at Passing Clouds. Little did we know that he – a young law student – and I – a sort of public servant – would end up producing bread in rural Victoria. Now John and Bronwyn supply bread into Melbourne and many locations along the Great Ocean Road, much to the delight of local residents and holidaymakers.

There is absolutely no excuse for not having a go at making these simple bread rolls. I promise you there is no scientific stuff here, and none of the so-called mysteries of bread-making.

500 g plain flour
1½ teaspoons dried yeast
a pinch of salt
50 g butter (or lard, which would be even better)
280 ml warm water, or enough to obtain a soft dough

simple bread rolls | makes 12 rolls or more

Put the flour, yeast, salt and butter in a bowl and gradually pour in the water, mixing as you do so with your hands. Work the mixture to a soft dough. At first it will stick to your hands, but as you work it, the dough will start to become smooth. Remember that you must knead the dough with some strength. Push it away from you firmly; do not pussy-foot around. After 5–10 minutes of determined kneading the dough should feel less sticky and begin to show some elasticity – when you pull it apart it will look like a see-through membrane. Form the dough into a ball and put into a large oiled bowl. Cover with clingfilm and leave to rest for an hour.
Preheat the oven to 220°C and line a tray with baking paper. Place the dough on your work surface and flatten it with your hands to a thickness of about 2 cm (do not use a rolling pin). Cut the dough into 12 pieces, or simply tear it with your hands without giving it any shape. Bake for 10 minutes until golden brown. If they're not quite ready, switch off the oven and leave the rolls there for a few more minutes.

sultana bread rolls The recipe is exactly the same as for the Simple Bread Rolls. All you have to do is soften 100 g of sultanas in a little water and add them to the dough when you mix it. Another nice alternative is to add 100 g roughly chopped walnuts. All these breads are very good on a cheese platter.

Another variation on the Simple Bread Roll recipe on page 50. The only difference is that you replace the butter with 50 ml extra-virgin olive oil.

rosemary focaccia | focaccia al rosmarino | serves 4

Follow the recipe and ingredients on page 50.

After the dough has rested and when you are ready to bake, use your hands to stretch out the dough to form a rough oval shape and transfer to the prepared baking tray. Poke your fingers into the surface of the dough to create dimples and stick in a few sprigs of dried rosemary. As you put the loaf in the oven sprinkle it lightly with water and a little rock salt. You can also add some pitted olives to the dough, in which case hold back on the rock salt. Bake for 10–15 minutes.

Hot focaccia is particularly good with Roasted Capsicums with Anchovy Cream (see page 5), and it is excellent with thinly sliced prosciutto and a few rocket leaves. I also like to serve it with fresh tomatoes and bocconcini, and all antipasto items.

the baker

Bill Mayne has been baking bread for our various establishments for the last three years. The sight of his bread coming out of the oven is one of the most sustaining moments in a profession where regularly one has to ask oneself if it is all worth it. The business of restaurants is very demanding. Enthusiasm and passion are the motivating forces for getting into it. Making a profit, sustaining the enthusiasm and the passion on a daily basis, year after year, is something else. People in our industry change jobs, or they move to another country, or change cooking styles, or they burn out. To remain stimulated and to stay out of the comfort zone is of paramount importance.

For me, to stay put in one physical location has demanded constant change within my organisation, but within that change I have also needed little pockets of certainty, small islands of security. Seeing the grapes ripening, the asparagus going to fern, the preserve kitchen handling the local fruits – oranges just picked on a frosty winter morning, for instance – are some of the most enduring images that give me that simple thing called the joy of life.

I gave up bread – much to my dislike – for more than three months to see what changes would occur to my body. For good measure, I eliminated pasta, rice, coffee, milk, desserts and all alcohol. You could say that I have tried a style of diet that excludes, beside sugar, all wheat-based carbohydrates. I can report that there has been no palpable change in my weight. The only time that my weight has reduced and stayed down, was after exercise – a damn awful lot of it.

I am now convinced, more than ever, that it is moderation in everything coupled with sensible exercising that keeps your body in a comfortable state.

Eat your bread, and if you want to know what's in it, make it yourself. I am not talking about bread mixes in the machine either – goodness knows how many preservatives are in there as well.

bill's toscana bread with rosemary and olives | makes 2 loaves

A note of warning about commercial flours: do not buy cheap home-brands for either pasta or bread-making. They have had most of their good properties removed. They can make an average scone, but are simply not strong enough to be worked into a bread mix. Lauckie is one company that makes very good flours for bread-making.

500 g baker's flour
10 g good quality salt
5 g dried yeast
325 ml lukewarm water
125 g chopped black olives
10 g fresh rosemary

Put all the ingredients into a large bowl and knead with a dough hook on a low speed until well combined. Change to high speed and knead the dough vigorously for 6–7 minutes until the dough is elastic. At this stage the dough is still rather wet. Don't worry, but cover and rest for at least 3 hours. Preheat the oven to 220°C, and line a tray with baking paper.
Shape the dough into 2 rough loaves. They will be rather 'free-form' as the dough is fairly moist (there is no need for any oil or butter in this dough). Cook for 20–24 minutes or until the loaves are cooked and sound hollow when you tap them on the underside.

simple white bread loaf
makes 2 loaves

Here is a really good recipe to get the hang of. You can use the same recipe to make pizza dough; just add 20 ml good olive oil to the mixture.

500 g strong white flour
10 g salt
5 g dried yeast
340 ml water

Put all the ingredients into a large bowl and knead with a dough hook on a low speed to bring the ingredients together. Change to a high speed and knead the dough vigorously for 6–7 minutes. You need to work the dough really well, so don't be afraid to give it a good belting. Rest the dough for a minimum of 3 hours in a moderately warm place.
Preheat the oven to 220°C and line a tray with baking paper. Divide the dough in half. Bake for 25 minutes, then remove from the oven and cool on a rack.

bruschetta

In my view, it is impossible to make acceptable bruschetta unless you use really good quality purchased bread or your own home-made bread. There is no point at all in making it with flaky, stale white bread, and unfortunately most bruschetta that is served comes drenched with poor-quality oil, flavourless tomatoes and too much garlic. What should be a simple and beautiful dish is turned into a nightmare.
So, first of all, make sure you use top-quality bread. Next, find a good way of grilling the bread – you can use the griddle plate on your barbecue or your gas stove. Rub the bread with only a little garlic and drizzle on the best olive oil you've got. If you want to top it with tomato, make sure the tomatoes are ripe and sweet, not acidic (and this rules out most commercially available tomatoes).

Give me minestrone any day, any time. I'll eat it hot in the winter, cold in the summer. My kids pack Nonna's minestrone into their school lunchbox at least once a week, while their mates get an assortment of soggy sandwiches or chips with gravy from the local take-away shop or school canteen. When will the government legislate against junk food in schools? What kind of democracy still allows these places to operate? There is nothing better than a hearty bruschetta, rubbed with a little garlic and drizzled with great olive oil, to complete the minestrone.

4 tablespoons extra-virgin olive oil
1 onion, peeled and finely chopped
1 carrot, peeled and diced
1 stick celery, finely chopped
4 potatoes, peeled and diced
salt and pepper
2 zucchini, diced
20 green beans, cut into 1 cm
    lengths
a good handful of peas, preferably
    fresh
3 ripe tomatoes, peeled and diced
2 litres chicken stock or water
freshly grated parmesan

Consider the ingredients listed bove as a guideline, rather than a hard-and-fast recipe.

Heat the olive oil in a large pot and sauté the onion, carrot and celery until they start to soften. Add the potatoes and season with salt and pepper. Then add the remaining vegetables and stir everything well. Add the chicken stock or water, then simmer for 1 hour with the lid askew until it thickens to a rich flavoursome soup.

If you like, you may add some white beans or chickpeas or lentils, but I prefer to cook them separately and add them later, with some of their cooking liquid, when the minestrone is nearly ready. Similarly, many minestrone soups include small pasta tubes and again, these should be cooked separately and added just before serving.

To serve, drizzle over a good slug of top-quality olive oil and, if you wish, some freshly grated parmesan.

It is worth letting bread go old just to make this soup, a starch-lover's paradise. And it absolutely cannot be made with 'white death', sliced supermarket white bread. However, when made with the right ingredients, the combination of bread and potato with peppery rocket, a hint of chilli and fragrant olive oil, it is a most rewarding dish.

500 g potatoes, peeled and thickly sliced

enough cold water to cover

salt

300 g stale bread

300 g rocket

100 ml extra-virgin olive oil

2 red chillies, sliced

3 cloves garlic, peeled and sliced

freshly grated pecorino or parmesan

bread soup with potatoes and rocket | serves 6 or more

Cover the potatoes with cold water and a little salt. Cook until soft. Add the bread and rocket, taste, and add more salt if necessary. You may also need to add a little more water, in which case do make sure it is hot, not cold.

Heat the olive oil in a small saucepan and gently fry the chilli and garlic for a few minutes. Discard the chilli if you do not like it, and pour the oil and garlic over the soup. Serve with freshly grated cheese.

Gnocchi is heavenly food. I have never understood why the Irish – people with a serious potato dependency problem – never developed gnocchi. One might have thought that the link with Catholicism – and therefore Italy – would have fostered an interest in gnocchi. Don't the Irish know that all Popes eat gnocchi?

Traditionally, only a relatively small amount of flour – just enough to hold it all together – goes into gnocchi.

2 kg old potatoes, or red potatoes like desirée
200 g plain flour, plus a little more for dusting
a touch of grated nutmeg
50 g parmesan, grated
a pinch of salt
2 eggs

potato gnocchi | makes enough for 10 serves

Boil the potatoes in their jackets until soft. Peel and push them through a potato ricer or a mouli and leave to cool. When almost cool, sprinkle the flour over the top and lightly work into the potato. Do not overwork the dough, just until the potato and flour are amalgamated.

Meanwhile, bring a small pot of salted water to the boil. You'll need it to test the gnocchi, to check if they hold together.

Break off a small piece of dough and use your hands to roll it out like a sausage no less than 1 cm thick. Cut into 1.5 cm pieces. Adjust the heat so the water is simmering and drop in the gnocchi. They should rise to the surface in a few minutes and not break up. If they do, add a little more flour to the dough, again being careful not to overwork. Cook the gnocchi in batches, allowing them room to swell. If cooking in large quantities, lift each batch out of the water with a slotted spoon, drain for a moment, tip into a buttered dish and keep warm. Serve the gnocchi with your chosen sauce. One of the best sauces, in my view, is made with gorgonzola (see page 220). Alternatively, my all-time favourite is gnocchi al ragu di carne, the classic Bolognese.

Pumpkin or *zucca* makes delightful gnocchi, or smaller ones called gnocchetti, which are fabulous with the simplest of all sauces – butter with sage and Parmigiano Reggiano. In this recipe the pumpkin must be roasted to concentrate the flavour and to dry it out. You need to prepare the gnocchi dough the day before you wish to eat it; the pumpkin needs to rest overnight to drain away as much moisture as possible.

2 kg pumpkin, cut into pieces, skin on (not butternut)

olive oil

salt and pepper

1 teaspoon sugar

leaves from 1 sprig rosemary

350 g ricotta

grated nutmeg

250 g plain flour

3 eggs, lightly beaten

50 g parmesan, grated

pumpkin gnocchi | serves 10 or more

Preheat the oven to 180°C. Rub the pumpkin pieces with a little oil and place, skin side down, in a baking tray with 1 cm of water. Season with salt and pepper and sprinkle with sugar and rosemary. Cover with a sheet of baking paper, then with a sheet of aluminium foil and bake until soft – the cooking time depends on how large your pumpkin pieces are.

Remove the pumpkin from the oven and use a spoon to scoop out the flesh. Push through a mouli or potato ricer and then transfer to a large sieve. Cover the top with clingfilm and rest in the fridge overnight to drain.

Push the ricotta through a mouli and add to the drained pumpkin flesh. Add a pinch of nutmeg, taste for salt, and add the flour. Add the eggs and the parmesan. The mixture should not be too wet.

Make the gnocchetti by quickly picking up the mixture with a teaspoon and pushing it into the boiling water with the index finger. As the gnocchetti come to the surface, gently scoop them out and place straight on the serving plate.

pasta

500 g strong flour

125 ml hot water

125 ml hot milk

sauce

4 tablespoons olive oil

1 small carrot, peeled and chopped

1 medium-sized brown onion, peeled and chopped

1 stick celery, chopped

1 clove garlic, chopped

1 lamb neck, trimmed of fat and cut into chunks

300 g stewing beef, preferably on the bone, cut into chunks

200 g pork shoulder, cut into chunks

100 ml red wine

salt and pepper

500 g or more good chopped peeled tomatoes

selection of fresh herbs, such as flat-leaf parsley, basil or a little thyme, tied in a bunch

freshly grated pecorino

One of the simplest pasta I know. It presents some difficulty in the preparation though, because it consists of only two ingredients – flour and liquid. It is all too easy to make a tough dough by not mixing in enough liquid. As with all traditional recipes, practice makes perfect.

The following recipe is strictly traditional, as is the accompanying sauce. I once prepared a dinner with Cheong Liew at the Grange Restaurant in Adelaide in which Cheong made perfectly soft, yet firm, cavatelli that he served with a veal, cucumber and tea sauce. I encourage you to be more adventurous too, and have therefore included a recipe for veal and cucumber sauce, inspired by Cheong, but made in a more Italian way.

cavatelli al pomodoro ricco | cavatelli with rich tomato sauce | serves 6

To make the Pasta, combine the flour, hot water and milk in a bowl or on the bench and mix until the dough is a smooth and elastic ball. The dough may take a little kneading to come together. Rest for 30 minutes at room temperature.

Flour the workbench well. Cut out a small piece of dough (about the size of a walnut) and roll it out into a long strip until it is about the thickness of a child's little finger. Cut into 2 cm lengths. Put your index and middle finger together, push in on a small piece of dough and drag it along the bench. The dough should almost curl in on itself, creating a hollow in the middle. Repeat with the rest of the dough.

To cook, drop the cavatelli into a large pot of boiling salted water. This dough needs to cook for 6–10 minutes, and the cavatelli will expand quite visibly. Do avoid overcooking, though. They should be soft, yet show a little resistance to the tooth.

To make the Sauce, heat the oil in a large heavy-based pan and fry the vegetables and garlic until they start to soften.

Add the meat and fry until they start to turn a light brown. Add the wine, season with salt and pepper, and add the tomatoes. Finally, add the herbs. Cook for at least 1½ hours. You may need to top up the cooking liquid with a little warm water from time to time.

At the end of the cooking time, remove the meat and the herbs. The meat will be pretty 'exhausted', but can still be eaten if you wish. This is a robust sauce, which should be tossed through the cavatelli and served with freshly grated pecorino.

This is almost two dishes in one, which is my favourite way of cooking. If you can get a tender veal rib eye, roast it, and serve it with the cavatelli and the same sauce.

300 g Cavatelli (see page 65)

freshly grated Parmigiano Reggiano, to taste

cucumber sauce

400 ml cream

4 tablespoons extra-virgin olive oil

4 very ripe tomatoes, chopped

1 continental cucumber, seeded and diced

salt and pepper

a little fresh basil

veal scaloppine

8 veal scaloppine (2 per person)

plain flour for dusting

4 tablespoons butter

4 tablespoons olive oil

8 sage leaves

50 ml white wine

salt and pepper

4 tablespoons cream

cavatelli with cucumber sauce and veal scaloppine | serves 4

To make the Cucumber Sauce, put the cream into a small saucepan and simmer gently until reduced by half.

Heat the oil in a non-stick frying pan and add the tomatoes in one go. Quickly remove the pan from the heat if it looks like it might catch fire. Return the pan to the heat and add the cucumber and cream. Add salt and pepper to taste. Simmer for a few minutes and add the fresh basil just before serving.

To cook the veal, first dust each piece in a little flour. Heat the butter and oil in a large non-stick frying pan. Add the sage leaves and veal, and brown lightly on one side. (You will probably have to cook the veal in two batches.) Turn the veal and cook for a few more minutes. Add the white wine and allow it to evaporate. Season with salt and pepper, then add the cream. Stir so that the veal is coated lightly with the cream.

Prepare the cavatelli according to the instructions on page 65. Cook the cavatelli in plenty of boiling salted water. When you are ready to serve, toss the cavatelli in the cucumber sauce and sprinkle with cheese. Carefully transfer the cavatelli to a large, hot serving platter. Arrange the veal scaloppine on one side and eat immediately.

Strozzapreti is a specialty from central Italy. Like cavatelli, it is a traditional pasta made without eggs, but it has a different shape. The dough is rolled through a pasta machine, a little at a time. As the sheet of pasta emerges from the machine, allow it to drop flat onto your work surface and cut it vertically into 1 cm strips. Each strip of pasta is then rolled between the palms of your hands to create a sort of corkscrew shape. Keep the pasta covered with a damp tea towel to stop it drying out, especially on hot days. The word 'strozzapreti' means 'priest stranglers'.

In the anti-clerical central part of Italy – once under the rule of the Papacy – the local priest was not a welcome guest! He was yet another mouth to feed on top of the already hungry family. A meal of flour and water was probably likely to 'choke' him.

It is traditional to serve strozzapreti with Bolognese sauce, but I encourage people to try this delicious sauce made with pork mince or sausage, some diced zucchini and a touch of saffron. Or try the Salame Sauce on page 23.

pasta

500 g strong white flour

about 1 cup hot milk

pork and saffron sauce

1 tablespoon olive oil

1 tablespoon butter

300 g Salame (page 23) or pork sausage mince

2 small zucchini, diced

125 ml cream

8 threads saffron, softened in a little warm water

salt and pepper

freshly grated parmesan

strozzapreti with pork and saffron sauce | serves 4

To make the Pasta, combine the flour and hot milk in a bowl or on the bench and mix until the dough is a smooth and elastic ball. The dough may take a little kneading to come together. Rest for 30 minutes at room temperature.

Set up your pasta machine. Cut off a small piece of dough, push it through setting 1, then setting 3, and finally, setting 7, until the pasta is about 2 mm thick.

Cut the pasta into strips of about 1 cm x 5 cm. Roll each strip between the palms of your hands so that each piece of pasta rolls in on itself like a little corkscrew.

To make the Sauce, heat the oil and butter in a heavy-based pan and fry the salame or pork mince, breaking up any lumps with a wooden spoon. Add the zucchini and sauté until the meat and zucchini are cooked through. Add the cream and saffron with its soaking liquid. Season with salt and pepper. Add a little more hot water if necessary.

Cook the strozzapreti in plenty of boiling salted water. When you are ready to serve, toss the strozzapreti in the pork and saffron sauce. If it seems a little dry, drizzle in a little extra-virgin olive oil. Serve with freshly grated cheese.

wheat for pasta Australian durum wheat in Italian-made pasta?

Out there in the back of New South Wales, Southern Queensland and parts of South Australia, Australians grow a hard wheat (hence the Latin durum), which makes excellent semolina. Milling this semolina properly – that is, turning wheat to flour with each particle a uniform size – is the second part of the pasta equation. Apparently Australia grows excellent durum wheat and knows how to turn it into proper semolina. Australian-made pasta – supermarket brand names – are now of very, very good quality.

I am reliably informed that the Italians are global procurers of semolina, as there is not enough land left for agricultural purposes in Italy. Australia, Canada and other countries are where they procure vast quantities of wheat which is turned into 'Italian pasta', which in turn is sold to the world – probably with some measure of European Economic Community subsidy, so that they can dump it on our supermarket shelves at prices the local manufacturers cannot compete with.

The future for Australian durum wheat – this is my pet dream – is to have the courage to do what we did with wine: take it to the whole world, especially to Asia, where consumers like pasta. It is not a silly dream: wheat is not labour-intensive, nor is milling it. Flour, or semolina, is transported to pasta factories in large tanks. There it is pumped into silos. From there it is channelled into the production line where computers regulate the flow of water and the correct mixing. It is then extruded through machinery, which give the pasta its appropriate shape. From there it is carefully dried and packaged. In the entire journey, not a single human hand has touched either the wheat or the flour. Sad in some ways, terribly efficient on the other.

Wheat has sustained many groups of people since farming began in the land between the Tigris and Euphrates Rivers. Durum wheat spread quickly and the Italians took to it with a vengeance. In Italy the wheat harvest is probably celebrated as much as the grape harvest, although without the same degree of bacchanalian revelry. Nevertheless, this precious grain is embedded in the cultural and gastronomic traditions of all regions of Italy.

Pastiera Napoletana is found around Naples, and I have embraced it because my own home town is surrounded by a huge wheat belt. Not only that, but citrus also pokes its orange head into the tart, and so we have a double whammy: Mildura citrus and Mallee wheat.

Admittedly, the preparation time required for this cake is long – you will need to start preparing it at least two days ahead of time – but the only difficult part is making sure the pastry is well made and properly cooked. Most people familiar with baking will find it a breeze.

I owe this perfect recipe to my friend, Loretta Sartori.

sweet shortcrust pastry

200 g unsalted butter

100 g caster sugar

1 egg (optional)

300 g plain flour

pastiera napoletana | wheat cake | makes 1 x 26 cm tart

tart filling

125 g whole wheat, soaked in cold water for 24 hours, or

   400 g canned cooked wheat (*gran pastiera*)

500 ml milk

1 cinnamon stick

1 vanilla bean, split and scraped

zest of 1 lemon

3 egg yolks

50 g caster sugar

300 g ricotta

80 g candied orange peel, diced

3 egg whites

2 tablespoons caster sugar

icing sugar

To make the Pastry, cream the butter and sugar together until the mixture is a pale yellow. Add the egg, if using, then fold in the flour, mixing quickly until it is just absorbed. Alternatively, add the flour to the creamed butter and sugar and pulse quickly until it is combined. Do not over-mix. The pastry will be soft and paste-like at this stage and requires chilling for 1 hour before use.

When ready to use the dough, remove the pastry from the refrigerator and turn it out onto a lightly floured work surface. Cut or break the dough into pieces and knead it lightly to soften. Roll out to an even thickness to ensure even shrinkage when baking.

To make the Filling, begin by soaking the wheat in cold water for 24 hours. The next day, bring a large pot of water to the boil with ½ teaspoon salt. Add the wheat and boil for 1 hour. Drain.

In a food processor, pulse the wheat to crack open the outer shell (the bran). Do not blend to a paste – the wheat should still be in quite large pieces, which helps it absorb the milk more readily as it cooks. Put the wheat into a heavy-based pan with the milk, cinnamon, vanilla bean and seeds and lemon zest. Cook slowly for 1–1½ hours, until the milk has been almost completely absorbed. Watch the pan and stir occasionally to make sure the milk does not catch on the bottom and burn. Remove from the heat and leave to cool. Refrigerate overnight, or for at least 8 hours, to allow the flavours to intensify and any excess milk to be fully absorbed.

The next day, preheat the oven to 180°C and line a baking sheet with baking paper. Cut out a 26 cm circle of sweet shortcrust pastry (to fit the base of the 26 cm springform tin), and bake on the lined baking sheet for 12–15 minutes, or until golden brown. Remove from the oven and leave to cool. Fit the pastry round into the greased springform tin and clip it tight. Press the remaining dough into the tin so that it fits into the sides. Ease the pastry up the sides to a height of around 5 cm. You will need to smear it onto the base to create a tight seal. The pastry shell should be around 4–5 mm thick. Trim the edges neatly.

Line the pastry with foil or non-stick baking paper, ensuring that the lining covers the base and comes up and over the sides. Fill the pastry shell with baking beans (or use dried beans or rice). Ensure that the bean filling supports the walls of the tart. Bake for about 30 minutes, or longer if you notice any opaque grey patches.

While the pastry is blind-baking, prepare the filling. In an electric mixer, whisk together the egg yolks and sugar. Change to a beater attachment and blend in the ricotta until it is well combined. Remove the aromatics from the cold cooked wheat and fold into the filling with the candied peel.

Whisk the egg whites until they form soft peaks. Add the 2 tablespoons caster sugar and continue whisking to form stiff peaks. Fold the egg whites into the ricotta filling and pour the mixture into the prepared pastry shell, spreading evenly. Return the tart to the oven and bake for 50–60 minutes. When cooked, the centre should be firm when pressed lightly. Leave to cool then dust with icing sugar. The tart should be served at room temperature.

Flour combined with eggs is one of the most successful culinary combinations. In a savoury sense, you get pasta. Add a little sugar and you get simple cakes, such as my favourite sponge cake. A sponge cake, flavoured with chocolate or dressed up with passionfruit or some fresh strawberries, served with a cup of tea or coffee, must be one treat that will never go out of fashion. The Italian tradition includes many simple treats based on eggs and flour, particularly in the biscotti family.

Egg-based pastas are easy to prepare and provide an endless source of simple pleasures. Making your own pasta fills you with a sense of achievement; preparing the filling or the sauce is equally rewarding. Traditionalists might well suggest classic fillings and sauces, but your imagination can take you to very special places. The main thing is to be familiar with pasta-making. It is easy as long as you do not give up at the first attempt. Like learning to ride a bike, you don't give up at the first fall!

500 g plain flour
5 large eggs

egg pasta | serves 6

This is a basic recipe, and like all basic recipes it may require adjustments here and there – a little more flour or a little more egg yolk may be needed, depending on the quality of the flour and the size of your eggs. Put the ingredients in a large bowl and start by mixing with a fork until roughly combined. Tip the dough out onto your work surface and continue to work by hand. In the good old days, Italian mammas had a special pasta board – really, just a simple board made out of a few slats of timber, but used specially for pasta-making. (A handyperson could knock something like this up in a few minutes.) The main thing to remember is never to wash the board.

Knead the dough vigorously until the flour and eggs are well combined to a smooth paste. It should be neither too hard or stiff, nor too soft. As you practise the art of pasta-making, your hands will learn how the dough is progressing and whether adjustments to the proportions are needed. After kneading, place the dough in a plastic bag for an hour to give it time to rest and relax at room temperature.

After the dough has rested you can roll it out to the required shapes. My advice is to buy a special pasta machine that makes light work of the job. (Of course you can roll it out with a rolling pin, but this is really quite tricky.) Another useful little tool is the small gadget used to cut out ravioli – it has a small wooden handle with a round crenulated wheel attachment that you roll across to the dough to cut out ravioli shapes. It is NOT the fancier contraption that you can buy to make six ravioli at a time.

Home-made pasta is perfect for making filled pasta to cook in a broth; popular varieties include tortellini and cappellacci. Then there are lovely little pasta butterflies to serve with delicate chicken rissoles.

You simply must make your own chicken stock, especially when making this dish; there is no excuse for not doing it. Chicken carcasses are cheap, a big pot is cheap and there is always space in the freezer compartment for frozen stock. I like the use of vegetables in stock. Do not listen to all the funny theories about stock. They are designed to put you off cooking.

200 g Egg Pasta (see page 77)

golden chicken stock

4 chicken carcasses or more (also add a few wings or feet)

1 large brown onion, cut in half

1 large carrot

2 sticks celery

a large pinch of salt

pasta di casa in brodo | pasta in a broth | serves 4

To make the Stock, just put all the ingredients in the largest pot you can buy (ideally it should be at least 10 litres – you will find many uses for it), cover with cold water and bring to the simmer very slowly. Do not let the stock boil fast. As it comes to the boil, some gunk and fat will rise to the surface. Skim this off and discard. As the stock simmers away you will need to keep skimming off the fat and impurities. Simmer for 2 hours and you will end up with a glorious golden stock that is full of flavour. Roll out the pasta, cut into ribbons and then into squares. Add the squares to the stock and cook for 3 minutes. Serve hot with grana cheese.

This is a similar soup to the Pasta di casa in brodo (see page 79), but here, the filled tortellini create lovely explosions of flavour in the mouth. Tortellini are a little fussy to make, and you can substitute good-quality bought ones. However, not all food can be simple; sometimes a serious cook has to rise to a challenge. Once mastered, the knack of preparing tortellini with a whole range of different fillings will enhance your overall ability in the kitchen and give you a real sense of pride. For Italians and other southern Europeans, quail are almost considered mythical birds; their meat is prized for its uniquely mild, gamey flavour. To replace the chicken with quail, increase the quantity to 150 g of quail meat.

1 tablespoon butter

1 tablespoon olive oil

1 small onion, chopped

100 g chicken meat, skin removed and meat diced

50 g prosciutto or good-quality ham, diced

1 egg

50 g Parmigiano Reggiano, grated

2 tablespoons fresh flat-leaf parsley

200 g Egg Pasta (see page 77)

egg wash made from 1 egg and 1 tablespoon water

1 litre Golden Chicken Stock (see page 79)

freshly grated Parmigiano Reggiano

half-moon tortellini with prosciutto and chicken | serves 6

Heat the butter and oil in a frying pan and gently sauté the onions until they soften. Add the chicken and prosciutto and fry with the onions until they are nearly cooked through (the chicken should still be a little pink). Set aside and leave to cool. Transfer the mixture to a food processor and pulse until a smooth paste. Add the egg, cheese and parsley, and pulse until well combined. If the mixture is too wet, you can thicken it with a few spoonfuls of fresh breadcrumbs. If it's too dry, slacken with a few spoons of cold chicken stock. Set aside.

To make the Tortellini, roll the pasta through a pasta machine, starting at setting number 1, then setting 5 and finally the last setting (8 or 9). Make sure you set the machine up on a lightly floured work surface to prevent the pasta sticking. Cut the pasta into 6 cm discs. You can use a special pastry cutter, or improvise. Place spoonfuls of the filling onto each pasta disc and lightly brush the edges with egg wash. Fold the pasta shapes into half-moons, sealing the edges well. To create the traditional tortellini shape, fold the edges together around your index finger and stick them together.

Bring the stock to the boil and drop in the tortellini. Lower the heat and simmer for about 4 minutes or until the tortellini are cooked through. Serve with freshly grated Parmigiano Reggiano.

Like most people, I like the faint gaminess of duck. Turning duck into a pasta sauce is a good way to use the bird and it makes a dish that is filling and economical. The addition of porcini mushrooms enriches the sauce, making it more silky and exotic.

You will probably need the meat from at least four duck marylands (jointed leg and thigh) for this dish. Don't use duck breast for this sauce as it tends to dry out too much. Reserve the duck bones to submerge into the sauce as it cooks for extra flavour.

strozzapreti with duck and porcini sauce | serves 4

4 tablespoons butter
4 tablespoons olive oil
2 small onions, peeled and chopped
1 carrot, peeled and chopped
1 stick celery, chopped
4 duck marylands, skinned and
    deboned, the flesh finely diced
50 ml white wine
4 fresh sage leaves
100 g chopped peeled fresh tomatoes
salt and pepper
20 pieces dried porcini mushrooms,
    softened in warm water
300 g Strozzapreti Pasta (see
    page 69)
freshly grated Grana Padano, to taste

Heat the butter and oil in a large heavy-based pan. Sauté the onions, carrot and celery until they soften. Add the duck and fry until it browns all over. Add the wine, duck bones, sage leaves and tomatoes, season with salt and pepper, and simmer very gently for 30 minutes.

Remove the porcini mushrooms from their soaking liquid, squeeze thoroughly and chop finely. Add the mushrooms to the sauce and simmer until it has reduced to a lovely thick consistency, a little like a Bolognese sauce. If it dries during the simmering process, add a few tablespoons of hot stock or water. You may also add a little of the porcini soaking liquid to the sauce for extra depth of flavour. Remove the duck bones before you dress the pasta.

Cook the strozzapretti in plenty of boiling salted water. When you are ready to serve, toss the strozzapretti in the sauce. Serve with Grana Padano.

ravioli di ricotta a spinaci
serves 4–5 as an entrée

It is best to prepare the ravioli just before you are ready to eat. When they dry out, the edges become hard and they take a long time to cook.

150 g fresh ricotta, as dry as possible
100 g spinach leaves, cooked,
    squeezed dry and chopped
50 g grated Parmigiano Reggiano or
    Grana Padano
a small pinch of freshly grated nutmeg
salt to taste
200 g Egg Pasta (see page 77)
1 egg, beaten

To make the Filling, mix the ricotta, spinach and cheese until well combined. Add the nutmeg and season with salt to taste.

When you are ready to eat, prepare the ravioli. Use a pasta machine to roll the pasta dough through the last or second-last setting (each machine is slightly different). The pasta sheet shouldn't be too thin or too thick. On one half of the pasta sheet drop teaspoons of the filling, evenly spaced, in two neat rows. Brush between the rows with the beaten egg and fold the other half of the dough over the mounds of filling. Carefully press the pasta together, expelling all the air. Use a ravioli cutter to cut into squares. Keep any trimmings and off-cuts; they can be frozen and are perfect to add to a minestrone. Cook the ravioli in plenty of boiling salted water. Serve with a fresh tomato sauce or a simple sauce made from melted butter and torn fresh sage leaves. Naturally, plenty of grated Parmigiano or Grana is a must.

The slightly gamey flavour of quail or pigeon ravioli, combined with a glass of Pinot Noir, is one of life's great gastronomic pleasures.

4 quail
200 g Egg Pasta (see page 77)
1 egg, beaten
freshly grated Parmigiano Reggiano
    or Grana Padano

sauce

1 tablespoon butter
1 tablespoon olive oil
1 onion, peeled and chopped
1 carrot, peeled and chopped
1 stick celery, chopped
a small bunch of mixed fresh herbs
salt and pepper
1 tablespoon butter
a few sage leaves

filling

1 teaspoon butter
1 teaspoon olive oil
½ onion, finely chopped
½ carrot, finely chopped
½ stick celery, finely chopped
a few sage leaves
a splash of white wine
½ cup grated Grana Padano

Begin by preparing the quail. Use a sharp knife to slice the breasts away from the quail and reserve for making the filling. Roughly chop the bird carcasses.

To make the Sauce, heat the butter and oil in a large pan and brown the quail bones. Add the vegetables and sauté for 5 minutes, or until the vegetables have softened and browned lightly. Add the herbs, season with salt and pepper, and pour on enough cold water to cover. Simmer until the stock reduces to a richly flavoured essence. Strain and reserve.

To make the Filling, coarsely chop the quail breasts. Heat the butter and oil in a heavy-based frying pan and fry the vegetables until they start to brown. Add the quail and sage, and season with salt and pepper. Cook for a few minutes, then add the wine and stir in well. Remove from the heat and allow to cool a little. Tip the filling into a food processor and pulse to a paste. Add the cheese and pulse briefly to combine.

Prepare the ravioli according to the method on page 82.

Cook the ravioli in plenty of boiling salted water. While the ravioli is cooking, finish the sauce. Melt the butter in a pan and throw in the sage leaves and the quail stock. Simmer to reduce a little. Drain the cooked ravioli and toss in the sauce. Serve with freshly grated Parmigiano or Grana to taste.

This is my favourite soup. Lentils with home-made pasta make a creamy, hearty soup for cold days. The pasta can be made well ahead of time and frozen (a flat pizza box is the perfect container). The soup can also be made in advance – in fact, I suggest making a large batch. It keeps for a few days and you can always have it twice in one week, can't you?
If you can, use Puy or the Australian small lentils for this dish; they hold their shape and will not disintegrate during cooking.

1 tablespoon butter

1 tablespoon olive oil

1 carrot, peeled and diced

1 small onion, peeled and diced

1 stick celery, diced

2 medium-sized potatoes, peeled and thinly sliced

200 g Puy lentils

2 litres Golden Chicken Stock (see page 79), warm

salt and pepper

200 g Egg Pasta (see page 77)

1 cup Italian-style tomato sauce

freshly grated parmesan

extra-virgin olive oil

pasta butterflies with lentils | serves 4

Heat the butter and olive oil in a large pan and sauté the carrot, onion and celery until they soften. Add the potatoes and stir well. Add the lentils and the warm stock and cook for about 25 minutes, or until the lentils are tender and the potatoes have broken down. Season with salt and pepper to taste. While the soup is cooking, prepare the pasta butterflies. Divide the pasta dough into thirds and roll them out to about 2 mm thickness on a lightly floured work surface. Keep the pasta sheets under a damp cloth to prevent them drying out. Use a crenulated ravioli cutter to cut the pasta into strips about 3 cm x 2 cm. With your thumb and index finger pinch each strip in the middle to create a butterfly (or bow tie) shape. Cook the pasta butterflies in plenty of boiling salted water.
When the lentils and potatoes are soft, add the tomato sauce – this enriches the soup. Add the cooked pasta butterflies to the soup, which should now have a nice thick consistency. Serve with freshly grated cheese and a good drizzle of extra-virgin olive oil.

ravioli con la zucca
serves 6

In some parts of Italy, pumpkin ravioli is made with the addition of sweet mustard fruits and crushed amaretti biscuits. The result is somewhat sweet and a sweet wine is usually needed to accompany it. There are several problems with this approach: I never know what to choose to eat after this dish and indeed, matching the whole meal sensibly is very difficult. I prefer to remove any sweetness from the pumpkin filling and keep these ravioli savoury.

150 g peeled pumpkin, roasted with a
    little garlic
50 g Parmigiano Reggiano or Grana
    Padano, freshly grated
a pinch of nutmeg
salt and pepper
200 g Egg Pasta (see page 77)

Mash the pumpkin with the cheese, nutmeg, salt and pepper. Prepare the ravioli according to the method on page 82. Serve with a simple sauce made from melted butter and torn fresh sage leaves. You can also enrich it with a splash of cream, if you like.

tagliolini con i calamari
serves 4

Tagliolini is like very thin fettuccine and is simple to prepare – just use the same dough as for fettuccine, and cut thinly with a knife. The tagliolini is delicious when simply dressed with a calamari sauce. The sauce can be red, when made with tomatoes, or black, when the calamari ink is added. I use calamari in this dish, but an astute foodie might use cuttlefish instead. Befriend a fishmonger, I say, and try the cuttlefish.

50 ml extra-virgin olive oil
1 small onion, peeled and chopped
1 small carrot, peeled and chopped
1 stick celery, chopped
2 cloves garlic, left whole
4 thin slices pancetta, chopped
4 medium-sized calamari or cuttlefish
    (avoid big fish), gutted and cut into
    small pieces
50 ml white wine
the ink sac of each cuttlefish
    (optional)
6 tinned tomatoes, chopped, and
    their juice
a pinch of chilli flakes
salt and pepper
freshly torn flat-leaf parsley
300 g Egg Pasta (see page 77)

Heat the oil in a large heavy-based pan and sauté the vegetables and garlic cloves until they start to soften. (The garlic can be removed later on, or left in, according to your preference.) Add the pancetta, calamari and white wine. Cook until the wine evaporates, then add the ink sacs, if using, followed by the tomatoes. Add the chilli and season with salt and pepper. Simmer gently for 45 minutes, adding a little water from time to time, if necessary. Add the parsley just before you toss the sauce with the tagliolini. When you are ready to eat, prepare the tagliolini. Use a pasta machine to roll out the pasta. Cut the rolled pasta sheet into manageable lengths, then roll up each length and slice thinly. Cook the tagliolini in plenty of boiling salted water until *al dente*. Drain well, then toss with the sauce.

spaghetti al sugo di pomodoro
serves 4

fettuccine ai funghi
serves 4

See the instructions on page 17 for making good, robust home-made spaghetti. The idea here is to work quickly. In fact, the correct term is spaghetti veloci – quick spaghetti – where the heroes are the tomatoes, the olive oil and the cheese.

4 tablespoons extra-virgin olive oil
2 cloves garlic, crushed
8 very ripe tomatoes (Roma are ideal), peeled, seeded and chopped
salt
300 g Home-made Spaghetti (see page 17)
basil leaves
freshly grated parmesan
extra-virgin olive oil

Heat the oil in a large pan and add the crushed garlic. Turn the heat to high and add the tomatoes (be careful to avoid any oil splashing and catching fire). The tomatoes should sizzle. Cook vigorously for a few minutes to reduce any liquid. Add salt to taste, then remove the pan from the heat.
When you are ready to eat, prepare the spaghetti according to the method on page 17. Cook in plenty of boiling salted water. Drain well. Throw the basil leaves into the sauce and toss with the spaghetti. Serve with freshly grated cheese and a drizzle of extra-virgin olive oil to taste.
Another nice variation to the basic recipe is to add a couple of anchovy fillets to the oil before the tomatoes. They add a lovely mellow flavour.

Ah, good old fettuccine! Of all home-made pastas, these are the easiest to make – all you have to do is put the sheet of pasta through the fettuccine cutter and bingo, there you have your fettuccine. There have been desperate occasions on holidays when I have resorted to rolling out the pasta dough with a wine bottle and cutting the fettuccine by hand with a sharp knife. The uneven thickness of the pasta dough produced by this rough-and-ready method made the fettuccine texturally much more exciting to eat.
If you are lucky to live in a temperate zone and you know how to pick mushrooms from the wild, you can make sublime Fettuccine ai Funghi.

2 tablespoons butter
1 tablespoon olive oil
1 small onion, peeled and chopped
1 clove garlic, chopped
200 g assorted mushrooms (the more the better; pine mushrooms are especially attractive when available)
40 ml white wine
salt and pepper
100 ml cream
3 tablespoons freshly torn flat-leaf parsley
300 g Egg Pasta (see page 77)
freshly grated parmesan

Heat the butter and oil in a heavy-based pan and sauté the onion until it starts to soften. Add the garlic and mushrooms, followed by the wine. Season with salt and pepper. Simmer until the mushrooms are soft and well amalgamated. The sauce can be prepared to this point ahead of time. Add the cream and parsley just before you toss the sauce with the fettuccine.
When you are ready to eat, prepare the fettuccine. Use a pasta machine to roll out the pasta then put it through the fettuccine cutter. Cook in plenty of boiling salted water. Drain well, then toss with the sauce. Serve with freshly grated cheese, to taste.

Home-made pasta is very porous and absorbs liquid very easily. To my mind there is nothing better than the delicious liquor that comes from various seafood, such as mussels, pipis (*vongole*), baby calamari rings, scallops and any white fish fillets – all flavoured with olive oil, garlic, white wine and flat-leaf parsley.

There is a freshness to this dish that is addictive. A range of fish and shellfish is readily available in Australia all year round, so substituting ingredients is very easy.

1½ tablespoons olive oil

1 clove garlic, chopped

4 small calamari, cut into small pieces

4 large prawns or 8 small ones, shelled

1 small fish fillet, cut into small pieces

30 ml dry white wine

8 mussels, briefly steamed until open

20 pipis, briefly steamed until opened

fresh flat-leaf parsley leaves, hand-torn at the last minute

300 g Egg Pasta (see page 77)

extra-virgin olive oil

tagliatelle al sugo di mare | tagliatelle with seafood | serves 4

Heat the oil in a non-stick pan, add the garlic and fry for a few seconds. Add the calamari, prawns, fish and wine, and cook for a few minutes. Next add the steamed shellfish. Cook for a few more moments and add the parsley just before you toss the sauce with the tagliatelle.

When you are ready to eat, prepare the tagliatelle. Use a pasta machine to roll out the pasta. Cut the rolled pasta sheet into manageable lengths, then roll up each length and slice thinly. Cook the tagliatelle in plenty of boiling salted water. Drain well, then toss with the sauce. Serve with a drizzle of extra-virgin olive oil. This sauce should be fairly liquid, but not too wet, and it should taste of the sea.

If you feel the need for some variety, you can embellish the recipe with finely diced zucchini or tomato, which should be added after the garlic, and before you add the seafood.

Blue swimmer crab is nearly always available, cooked or raw. Raw is better, but the crab must be fresh. Steam fresh crab for 7–8 minutes and pick out the meat. Spaghetti can be made by pushing the pasta sheet through the spaghetti cutter on your machine (see page 17), or use a sound commercial brand.

50 ml olive oil

4 Roma tomatoes, peeled, seeded and chopped

1 clove garlic, finely chopped

200 g (or more!) crab meat

300 g Egg Pasta (see page 77)

freshly torn flat-leaf parsley or basil

salt and pepper

extra-virgin olive oil

spaghetti con granchio | spaghetti with crab | serves 4

Heat the oil in a non-stick pan and cook the tomatoes and garlic for 3–4 minutes. Add the crab meat. Cook the pasta in plenty of boiling salted water until *al dente*. Drain well, then toss with the sauce. Add the parsley, season to taste with salt and pepper, and finish with more extra-virgin olive oil.

I like this humble dish so much I always show it at cooking demonstrations. Mind you, I don't get to see it on other people's menus often, so perhaps I have not been very convincing. Believe me, it is a treat.

You can also make this dish with good-quality bought orecchiette, but I like home-made pasta, and the structure and texture of pappardelle. You need a fair amount of olive oil for this dish, and the greener and fresher it is, the better tasting the final dish.

300 g Egg Pasta (see page 77)
100 ml extra-virgin olive oil
1 clove garlic, chopped
1 small fresh chilli, not too hot, sliced
4 anchovy fillets
200 g broccoli, cooked to break-down point
shaved pecorino, to taste

pappardelle con i broccoli | pappardelle with broccoli | serves 4

First make the pappardelle by rolling out the pasta through to the second last setting of the machine; this pasta should not be too refined. Cut the pasta sheets to lengths of about 30 cm, then roll each piece on itself and cut the pappardelle at least 2–3 cm wide. Or you can cut the sheet lengthwise with a ravioli cutter to get the crenulated edges. Keep well-floured to prevent sticking.

Heat the olive oil in a non-stick pan and fry the garlic, chilli and anchovies. Add the broccoli and smash with a wooden spoon until all the ingredients are well integrated.

Cook the pappardelle in plenty of boiling salted water. Drain well, then toss with the sauce. Stir in the cheese. This dish should be tasty and unctuous, in the best possible sense of the word. You can even add more oil, if you like.

fettuccine al formaggio
serves 4

The texture of fettuccine is perfectly suited to a cheese sauce – and there are so many wonderful cheeses to choose from. A blue cheese from the gorgonzola family, perhaps, or one of the lovely Aussie blues – with a little mascarpone and the usual grated parmesan – will make a creamy and sticky sauce, which can come to the rescue on any cold night.

30 g butter
100 g mascarpone
80 g blue cheese
300 g Egg Pasta (see page 77)
freshly ground black pepper
freshly grated parmesan

Melt the butter and mascarpone in a heavy-based pan. Add the blue cheese and stir to amalgamate.
When you are ready to eat, prepare the fettuccine. Use a pasta machine to roll out the pasta, then put it through the fettuccine cutter. Cook in plenty of boiling salted water. Drain well, then toss with the sauce. Serve with black pepper and parmesan.

cannelloni di ricotta e spinaci
serves 6 or more

Some people might think cannelloni are a little fussy to make, when everything needs to be done in no time at all. But to my mind, this remains a classic dish, no matter what. When prepared with care, the cannelloni are tasty and deliciously soft.

300 g spinach (or, if you are in a
    hurry, frozen spinach)
1 tablespoon butter
500 g fresh ricotta
2 eggs
100 g grated Parmigiano Reggiano,
    plus an extra handful
salt and pepper
200 g Egg Pasta (see page 77)
béchamel sauce
150 g unsalted butter
100 g plain flour
1.5 litres hot milk
freshly grated nutmeg

To make the Béchamel Sauce, melt the butter and mix with the flour. Cook a little but without browning. Stir in the milk, bit by bit, mixing with a wooden spoon. Initially the mixture will be like a gluggy lump but as you add the milk it will break down more and more. Cook it gently for 20 minutes or more, taking care that it does not stick to the bottom of the pan. Add nutmeg to taste. This recipe should yield a fairly soft sauce, which is what we want. If it is too thick add more milk or water. If you think you have some lumps in it, pass it through a fine sieve and everything will be all right.

Bring a large pot of salted water to the boil and blanch the spinach, drain and squeeze dry. (I far prefer using proper bunches of spinach, rather than ready-trimmed little spinach leaves.) Roughly chop the spinach.
Heat the butter in a large pan and briefly sauté the spinach. In a separate bowl, combine the ricotta, eggs, grated cheese, salt and pepper. Stir in the spinach and mix well.
Roll the pasta through the last setting on your pasta machine and cut the sheets into sections about 10 cm wide. Cook the pasta sheets in plenty of boiling salted water, then plunge into a bowl of cold water. When cold, place on a tea towel to dry.
When you are ready to cook the cannelloni, preheat the oven to 180°C. Spread a third of the béchamel sauce over the bottom of a baking dish. Lay the pasta sheets on a work surface and spoon some filling along the centre of each. Roll up to form fat cigars. Arrange the filled cannelloni in the baking dish and spread the remaining béchamel sauce over the top. Sprinkle with the extra cheese and bake for around 15 minutes until the top is bubbling and golden.
If you like, you can introduce a tomato element to this dish. Spoon a few tablespoons of home-made tomato sauce over the béchamel before topping with the extra grated cheese. Don't overdo the tomato though, as the acid can rather dominate the flavour.

sponge biscuits
makes about 25

These biscuits are necessary for the preparation of tiramisu (see page 211). You are almost certainly familiar with this dessert, but I assure you it is more satisfying to make it with your own biscuits instead of buying them.

4 egg yolks
2 tablespoons caster sugar
40 g plain flour, sifted
40 g cornflour, sifted
4 egg whites
2 tablespoons caster sugar (for meringue)
80 g caster sugar

Preheat the oven to 180°C and line a baking tray with non-stick baking paper. Whisk the egg yolks with the caster sugar until thick and pale. Sift the flour and cornflour together.

In a clean bowl, whisk the egg whites to soft peaks, then gradually add the caster sugar and continue whisking to form a glossy meringue. Fold a third of the meringue into the yolks, then fold the remaining meringue and flours into the mix in alternate lots. Mix gently, stopping once the ingredients are combined.

Transfer the mixture to a piping bag fitted with a plain round 1 cm nozzle. Sprinkle 80 g caster sugar over the bottom of another baking tray.

Pipe the sponge fingers onto small strips of non-stick baking paper. Carefully lift each piped biscuit on its piece of paper and invert onto the sugared tray. Once the surface is coated with sugar, place the biscuit, sugared side up, on the prepared baking tray and bake for 15–25 minutes, depending on how dry you like the biscuits.

sponge cake
makes 1 x 26 cm cake

At its simplest, a sponge cake, with the addition of seasonal fruits or berries, some cream or a sweet icing, is one of the delights of home cooking. Even if a sponge comes out of the oven with some imperfection, the fragrant combination of eggs, flour and sugar is enough to get you over the line. With these ingredients you cannot go really wrong.

A custard filling is wonderful with a sponge cake. You might also add some strawberries, either between the layers of the cake or on the side. For something a little more exotic, sprinkle the sponge with a liqueur like Strega or Grand Marnier. Fresh sponge does not need much, but if it is a day or so old it is better to moisturise the sponge with a sugar syrup.

This easy sponge is the basis for countless desserts.

sponge
100 g plain flour, sifted
50 g cornflour, sifted
5 medium-sized eggs, separated
100 g caster sugar
custard
500 ml milk
100 g caster sugar
1 vanilla bean (optional)
3 egg yolks
50 g cornflour

Preheat the oven to 180°C and butter and lightly flour a 26 cm cake tin.

To make the Sponge, first combine the sifted flours in a bowl.

In another mixing bowl, whisk the eggs whites to soft peaks, then gradually add the sugar and continue whisking to form a glossy meringue. Leave the motor on a medium speed and add the yolks one by one, mixing until combined. Gently fold in the combined flours.

Pour the batter into the prepared tin and bake for 35 minutes. Remove from the oven and leave to cool.

To make the Custard, put the milk into a large saucepan with half the caster sugar and the vanilla bean and bring to the boil.

Meanwhile, whisk together the egg yolks and the remaining sugar, then add the cornflour to form a paste. Carefully pour a little hot milk onto the yolk paste, whisking well to incorporate. Continue slowly adding the hot milk until half is used. Remove the vanilla bean, split it and scrape the seeds into the remaining milk. Bring the milk back to the boil and pour it onto the yolk mixture. Tip the whole lot back into the saucepan over a medium heat. At this point the custard will thicken quickly, so work fast and continue whisking until it returns to the boil. Cook for a few minutes to make sure the flour has lost its raw taste, then pour the custard into a clean bowl and cover the surface with clingfilm.

Refrigerate until it has cooled completely. When you are ready to fill the sponge, beat the custard briefly using an electric beater to ensure it is really smooth.

When the cake is completely cool, split in half and fill with lavish amounts of custard.

As well as flour and eggs, these biscotti contain almonds. Where I live, and thanks to the water of the Murray River, I am surrounded by a whopping 30,000 acres of almond trees in full production. Almonds thrive in dry, semi-arid zones, provided water is available for irrigation. The sight of countless acres of almond trees in blossom against a pale blue, late-winter sky is one of nature's best scenes. It takes the help of 40 semitrailers of bee hives to cross-pollinate all these trees. It is worth a trip to see, from wherever you live. In these biscotti the almonds add crunch and a subtle aroma. I also like the use of olive oil in this recipe.

1 egg
1 egg yolk
125 g caster sugar
½ tablespoon olive oil
150 g self-raising flour
50 g almonds, roasted and roughly chopped
½ teaspoon anise seeds (optional)

biscotti di prato | makes 30–40

Preheat the oven to 170°C and line a baking tray with non-stick baking paper.
Whisk together the egg, egg yolk and sugar until thick and pale. Add the oil to the eggs.
Combine the flour, almonds and anise, if using. Add the flour mixture to the eggs and stir until a sticky dough forms.
Dust your work surface well with flour and roll out the dough into pencil-shaped lengths. Place the pastry lengths on the prepared baking tray, allowing space in between for the biscuits to expand.
Bake for 15 minutes until golden. Cool and store in an airtight container.

lemon cake
serves 10

Lemons are another essential item in Mediterranean cooking in both savoury and sweet dishes. Here is a recipe for a simple lemon cake from my mother-in-law, who always bakes for our family get-togethers.

125 g unsalted butter
220 g caster sugar
1 tablespoon finely grated
   lemon zest
2 eggs
150 g self-raising flour, sifted
75 g plain flour, sifted
125 ml milk
125 lemon juice
60 g caster sugar, extra

Preheat the oven to 180°C. Grease a high 22 cm round cake tin and line the base with baking paper.
Beat the butter, sugar and zest until light and fluffy. Add the eggs, one at the time, beating until well combined. Add the sifted flours, alternating with the milk. Pour the mixture into the prepared tin and cook for 45 minutes until the top is golden and a cake-tester or skewer inserted in the middle comes out clean.
Mix the lemon juice and sugar together and pour over the cake while still hot. Let it rest for some time in the tin and turn out to cool on a wire rack.

crêpes with orange segments, pears or apples | makes 4

Another delightful combination of flour and eggs – with milk also playing a major role. When crêpes are well made, they are delicious. What I really like in this recipe is the citrus butter that melts into a delicious syrup. Oranges are one of the most beautiful and versatile ingredients in most major cuisines of the world. I am lucky to live in the orange capital of Australia, and my walks through the countryside on crisp winter mornings inevitably end up with a feed of either oranges, grapefruit or mandarins. Nothing is more juicy and fragrant than a piece of fruit picked straight from its tree!

citrus butter
50 g unsalted butter, at room
   temperature
50 g caster sugar
juice and grated zest of 1/2 orange
optional dash of Grand Marnier
fruit
4 blood oranges
1 tablespoon butter
1 tablespoon caster sugar
crêpes
1 egg
65 g plain flour
a pinch of salt
120 ml milk
1 tablespoon softened butter
grated zest of 1/2 orange
1 teaspoon Grand Marnier
2 teaspoons caster sugar
butter for frying

To make the Citrus Butter, beat all the ingredients together. It is important that the butter be at room temperature: if it is too hard it will not cream with the other ingredients; too soft and it risks separating when you add the orange juice. Keep at room temperature while you prepare the crêpes.
To make the Crêpes, place the egg, flour and salt in a bowl and whisk lightly. Slowly add the milk and butter. Whisk in the zest, liqueur and sugar. Heat a heavy-based non-stick crêpe pan over a medium heat. Brush with a little butter and ladle on enough batter just to coat the bottom of the pan thinly. There is no secret here with making crêpes, just good, old-fashioned practice.
For the Fruit, peel the oranges and use a sharp knife to remove the membrane and carefully slice out each segment between the membranes. If you are using apples or pears, peel and thinly slice.
Heat the butter and sugar in a heavy-based frying pan and toss the fruit for a few minutes until lightly caramelised.
To serve, spread a little citrus butter over the crêpes and top with the warm fruit.

I galani are fried pastries found all over Italy under many different names. In Venice and in the Veneto the word *galani* derives from the sails of certain Venetian ships, so the name is steeped in maritime history. In other parts they are called *chiacchiere*, or gossips, because you eat them as you chat over a cup of coffee. In other parts of the country they are also known as lies, because a chat leads to gossip and gossip inevitably leads to lies.

I galani are a carnival-time treat – which is a time when you can play tricks and also tell lies – but in Australia, where this festivity does not exist, you can eat them at any time. They are excellent with zabaglione.

1 teaspoon baking powder

375 g plain flour

30 g caster sugar

40 g butter

juice of 1/2 orange

zest of 2 oranges

a dash of grappa or Cointreau

2 eggs

oil for deep-frying

plain flour for dusting

caster sugar or icing sugar

i galani | makes about 60, depending on how you cut the pastry

Mix the baking powder with the flour and sugar on the workbench. Rub in the butter. Make a well in the centre of the flour and pour in the juice, zest, brandy and eggs. Slowly bring the flour into the centre, mixing to incorporate. Continue until a dough is formed. Knead well for at least 5 minutes, wrap in clingfilm and rest for an hour. If the kitchen is cool, do not refrigerate.

Divide the dough into 3–4 pieces. They can be rolled by hand, but I find it easier to roll through a pasta machine. Working with a piece of dough at a time, press the dough in the flour and pass it through the machine at the widest setting. Dust well with flour again, fold in half and pass it through. Repeat with the rest of the dough. If the dough is awkward to handle, cut into manageable lengths. Ensure all the pieces are rolled through at the first thickness. Continue passing the dough through on each of the subsequent thicknesses until you get to the second last setting. By this stage you will have very long sheets of dough about 1.5 mm thickness. Cut in half to make them easier to handle.

Cut the dough into 3–4 cm strips across the width.

To cook, heat the oil in a deep pan to about 175°C. Use a scrap of dough to test the heat: the dough should turn golden in about 30 seconds. Cook the pastries, 2 or 3 at a time, depending on the size of your pan. Once the pastry is golden and puffed up, turn it over to cook the other side. Remove from the oil and drain on kitchen paper. Sprinkle immediately with caster sugar or sifted icing sugar.

These little self-saucing puddings are a wonderful dessert for chocolate lovers, and I've included the recipe here even though they contain no flour. Call it a cookbook writer's privileges! The home cook must be prepared to take a risk, because this is one of those desserts that is really better suited to a restaurant environment where the conditions never change and daily practice ensures a fairly even result. At home you must experiment until you get everything right.

300 g best chocolate (85 per cent cocoa)

150 g unsalted butter

20 ml brandy

6 eggs, separated

90 g caster sugar

chocolate tortino | makes 8

Preheat the oven to 210°C. Butter 8 metal dariole moulds and dust each very lightly with flour.
Melt the chocolate, butter and brandy in a bowl set over simmering water, then leave to cool to room temperature.
In a separate bowl, beat the egg yolks and sugar together until they are pale and doubled in volume.
Whisk the egg whites to stiff peak stage and gently fold into the egg yolks. Fold in the cooled chocolate (it must be at room temperature, or it will harden) until evenly combined. Pour into the dariole moulds and bake for exactly 9 minutes. The puddings should be firm on the outside and still undercooked in the centre.
These chocolate tortino are very rich and really just need a little whipped cream on the side. If you prefer, you could also serve them with vanilla ice-cream or a light custard cream.

polenta e riso

polenta and rice

polenta is ground maize. Maize came from the Americas and therefore, like potato, tomato, chilli and eggplant, is regarded in old Europe as a post-Colombian ingredient. Imagine life in Europe before Christopher Columbus brought back the spud and the ubiquitous tomato! Life without gnocchi and *spaghetti al pomodoro* is simply not imaginable.

Polenta has a multitude of uses, both savoury and sweet. As I remember it, polenta was always white, that is, made from white maize. It is available here in Australia in specialist food stores and is worth pursuing. White polenta is delicate, creamy and finely textured.

White polenta suits fish-based recipes, such as cuttlefish or calamari cooked in their own ink or a tomato-based fish stew – see some of the following recipes – or white meats like rabbit and olive stews.

Yellow polenta is coarser, gutsier and better suited to strong meat-based stews. Braised lamb and peas is an ideal polenta dish, as is braised lamb neck or ossobuco. Indeed, anything with strong flavour and loads of sauce.

Both white and yellow polenta are a vegetarian delight, with braised veggies or melted cheese such as gorgonzola (see the chapter on cheese).

I grew up with polenta, and am one of a generation born on the land of polenta that remembers every single part of the horrendous cycle of maize farming. The very thought of a sharp blade of maize leaf sliding along your neck, as one is working through a vast field of maize, evokes a sense of irritation and pain to this day.

The thing to ponder is that the background of polenta is partially connected to the development of Australia: hordes of people with nothing to eat but polenta decided to look for a better future in Australia. Many of them went into the building trades and agriculture from Victoria to Queensland, from NSW to WA, and now some of the most successful Australian building firms are run by the children of people who had nothing much to eat other than polenta. Other children of that generation became lawyers, business people and high-ranking officers of the Australian government.

So this chapter is for them, and to remind them, if ever they read this book, of where they came from.

Like porridge, white polenta is delicious when cooked in hot milk and drizzled with honey or jam. It is an unusual breakfast dish for the Aussie palate, which is the very reason I am including it here.

1 litre milk
1 tablespoon caster sugar (optional)
1 cup white polenta or more
honey or jam, to taste
extra hot milk, to taste

white polenta with milk and honey | serves 4

Put the milk and sugar in a small saucepan and bring to the boil. Carefully pour on the polenta in a slow steady steam, whisking to avoid lumps. Lower the heat and cook very gently for at least 20 minutes, stirring all the time. The polenta will plop as it's cooking, and you need to beware of hot polenta splatters. The quantities indicated will make a soft polenta – you need to experiment to find the consistency you like: add a little more polenta if you like it thicker.
When cooked, divide the polenta between 4 bowls and serve with honey, and extra hot milk to taste.

50 ml extra-virgin olive oil

1 small onion, peeled and chopped

1 small carrot, peeled and chopped

1 stick celery, chopped

2 cloves garlic, left whole

4 slices pancetta, chopped

4 medium-sized calamari or cuttlefish (avoid big fish), gutted and cut into small pieces

50 ml white wine

the ink sac of each cuttlefish (optional)

6 tinned tomatoes, chopped, and their juice

a pinch of chilli flakes

2 bay leaves

salt and pepper

freshly torn flat-leaf parsley

1 litre hot water

1½ cups white polenta

white polenta with black cuttlefish | serves 6

Heat the oil in a large heavy-based pan and sauté the vegetables and garlic cloves until they start to soften. (The garlic can be removed later on, or left in, according to your preference.)
Add the pancetta, calamari and white wine. Cook until the wine evaporates, then add the ink sacs, if using, followed by the tomatoes. Add the chilli, bay leaves, and season with salt and pepper. Simmer gently for 45 minutes, adding a little water from time to time if necessary. Add the parsley.
Put the hot water in a large pot and lightly salt. Gradually add the polenta, stirring all the time on a low heat, until the polenta loses its grainy taste, about 30 minutes. You don't have to be stirring all the time as with a risotto; an occasional stir should be sufficient.
When ready, serve with the cuttlefish.

1 litre hot water
salt to taste
1½ cups yellow polenta

Put the hot water in a large pot and lightly salt. Gradually add the polenta by allowing it to fall from your hand from above the pot like sand through your fingers. If the water is not boiling, you will be able to stir in all the polenta without lumps forming. As the temperature rises, the flour will integrate with the water and thicken. Stir all the time, and if you have used too much of the flour and the mixture is too thick, add a little water. I taste for salt and perhaps add some parmesan cheese. When the polenta is smooth and does not taste of raw maize, it is ready.

You can use this sloppy polenta with anything that has been braising for a while: chicken, beef and fish stews, vegetables and mushrooms, grilled sausages, quails, liver cooked with onions and so on.

Alternatively, pour the polenta into a flat baking dish where it will cool and become firm. At that point it can be grilled or oven baked.

As a grilled slice, polenta will accompany many creative Australian dishes – as a base for fried eggplant slices, goat's cheese, rocket, artichokes, prosciutto and so on. For me grilled polenta is good with either baked or fried fish, baccalà mantecato or lumps of parmesan. Baked polenta can be dressed with cheese, roasted capsicums and fine salame or pancetta.

After you have poured the hot polenta into a tray some will remain stuck to the sides of the pot. Let it dry, even for a day, and peel these skins off. They are delicious with parmesan.

The combination of sausages and polenta must be as old as cooking itself. The sausages can be cooked on a barbecue or, for a richer and more wintry dish, braised in a rich tomato sauce. If grilled or barbecued, it is best to serve them with a simple salad – radicchio, fennel or rocket are all good – or with spinach. Good continental-style pork sausages are best for this rustic dish. It sounds easy, but they can be harder to find than you might think. Too many butchers jazz up their sausages with weird additions and flavour combinations or mince the meat too finely. Look for a straightforward version, simply seasoned with salt and pepper and with good coarsely ground visible chunks of meat, such as those sold by Jonathan's in Melbourne. This is more a meal suggestion than an actual recipe. Most people will be comfortable with grilling or barbecuing sausages. If you are braising them, I suggest you prick the skins and plunge the sausages in boiling water for a few minutes to release some fat – if that worries you. Otherwise plunge straight into a rich tomato sauce and cook gently until done. Serve with soft-cooked yellow polenta.

yellow polenta with chicken livers and spinach | serves 4

Here is another inexpensive dish that is worth revisiting. The availability of good chickens now means that excellent chicken livers are easier to find.

100 g butter
30 ml olive oil
400 g chicken livers, trimmed of sinew
6 sage leaves
salt and pepper
4 large handfuls fresh spinach
1 teaspoon preserved lemon, chopped
1 quantity Polenta (page 112)
freshly grated parmesan (optional)

Heat half the butter and all of the oil in a non-stick frying pan. Add the chicken livers and sage leaves, and season with salt and pepper. Fry gently until the livers are just cooked pink. Be careful not to overcook. In another saucepan, heat the remaining butter, add the spinach and cook quickly over a high heat. Add the preserved lemon and season to taste. Stir the spinach into the cooked chicken livers and stir to combine. Leave behind as much of the excess water from the spinach as you can. Serve on a bed of soft-cooked yellow polenta, perhaps enriched with a sprinkle of parmesan.

As with the Fettuccine ai Funghi (page 87), this wonderful recipe relies on a variety of exotic mushrooms, which can be hard to obtain in many Australian cities. If you live in South Australia and have access to pine mushrooms or field mushrooms, then give yourself a treat and use them to make this dish. Otherwise, the usual range of commercially cultivated mushrooms will do more than adequately.
Polenta with funghi can be eaten as a vegetarian dish or it can be served as an accompaniment to a robust roasted meat dish.

yellow polenta with funghi serves 4

50 g butter
50 ml extra-virgin olive oil
3 cloves garlic, chopped
1.5 kg assorted mushrooms (include as many good wild ones as you can find)
salt and pepper
50 ml white wine
leaves from 1 bunch flat-leaf parsley
grated lemon zest (optional)
1 quantity Polenta (page 112)
4 tablespoons mascarpone

Heat the butter and oil in a heavy-based frying pan. Add the garlic and mushrooms, and season with salt and pepper. Add the white wine and simmer. The mushrooms will release a lot of water as they cook, so simmer gently until most of the liquid evaporates. When ready to serve, sprinkle on the parsley leaves and a little grated lemon zest, if using. For a richer dish you can add some chopped bacon. You can also enrich the mushroom flavour with a couple of tablespoons of commercially available veal or beef jus.
Serve on soft-cooked yellow polenta with a little mascarpone.

Here is treat that will either appeal or not. I have given up trying to convert people, although I do find that most people like tripe once they've tasted it. I frequently serve this dish in my restaurant as a 'special', over and above the menu of the day.

You can buy tripe in several ways: either uncooked, which takes a long time to cook, or part-cooked, which tends to be a more acceptable option. The softness of tripe goes exceptionally well with polenta.

50 ml olive oil

2 onions, peeled and chopped

2 carrots, peeled and chopped

2 sticks celery, chopped

200 g pork belly, cut into several pieces (optional)

1 kg part-cooked tripe, blanched in boiling water

80 ml red wine

600 g tomatoes, peeled

a pinch of chilli powder

salt and pepper

200 g cooked borlotti beans (optional)

1 quantity Polenta (see page 112)

yellow polenta with braised tripe | serves 4–6

Heat the oil in a large heavy-based casserole and sauté the onions, carrots and celery until they soften and brown. If using the pork belly, sauté it with the vegetables.

Slice the tripe into strips about 5 mm wide, although you'll find the length will vary. Add the tripe to the casserole with the wine. Simmer until the wine has evaporated, then add the tomatoes and seasonings and simmer gently with the lid askew for 1½ hours, or until the tripe is creamy and soft. Add the borlotti beans, if you're using them, towards the end of the cooking time.

Make the polenta following the recipe on page 112, and serve with the tripe.

yellow polenta with braised lamb
serves 8

In my view, the entire population of Australia should be forced to consume a diet of braised lamb shoulder and necks! Lamb and other ovine are the specialty food of Australia and there is life beyond lamb roast or rack of lamb.

This recipe of braised lamb is a rich stew of the lesser parts, complemented by creamy yellow polenta. It is so easy to cook and is tasty and relatively cheap. Braises and stews are not fashionable food in Australia these days – but they are great on cold days and easy to prepare.

1.2 kg lamb shoulder, cut into 2 cm cubes
plain flour for dusting
olive oil for frying
2 brown onions, peeled and chopped
2 carrots, peeled and chopped
2 sticks celery, chopped
6 cloves garlic, peeled and left whole
a small bunch of rosemary and sage, tied together
100 ml red wine
2 potatoes, peeled and diced
salt and pepper
600 g Italian tomatoes, peeled and chopped
1½ quantities Polenta (page 112)
grated zest of ½ orange
grated zest of ½ lemon
1 tablespoon finely chopped flat-leaf parsley

Dust the lamb with flour. Heat the oil in a large frying pan – preferably non-stick – and fry the lamb in small batches until golden brown. Set aside. Heat a little more oil in a large casserole pan and fry the onions, carrots, celery and garlic until they begin to soften and brown. Return the lamb to the pan with the herbs and stir well. Add the wine and simmer until it evaporates. Add the potatoes and season with salt and pepper. The potatoes are a kind of thickener in this dish – they will break down and almost disappear into the sauce by the end of the cooking time. Add the tomatoes and cook slowly for 1½ hours or more on the stove top. The sauce should deepen in colour and thicken. If it is too thick, thin with a little water or stock.

Soft-cooked yellow polenta is the perfect accompaniment to this rustic braised dish. It's certainly preferable to the awful practice of serving casseroles and stews with long-grain rice. Sprinkle on a little grated orange and lemon zest and chopped parsley as you serve.

polenta and farmed rabbit
serves 4–6

Only a few years ago many Australians were repulsed by the idea of eating rabbit. Vivid memories of rabbit fences, disease and harsh years of drought and depression made rabbit a most detested food. Mercifully memories of the depression years are waning and the farmed rabbit is marching on, becoming more readily available and increasingly accepted on restaurant tables.

In Europe I was accustomed to farmed rabbit or hare. A hare, or indeed anything from the wild, was very sought after. My cousin Giulio, a keen hunter, and a proud railway man, nearly finished his long career at the service of the Italian Rail in disgrace because of a hare. He was driving a small train on the familiar lunchtime student run between two cities when suddenly a hare appeared on the tracks. His predatory instincts prevailed and he hit the animal. 'Great' – he said to his mate – 'let's stop the train and get dinner!' Unfortunately, on that simple old type of train, if you open one door they all open. There was a blind man on board. When the train came to a stop, his dog thought they had arrived at the station, so he led his master out. And the poor bloke fell over, luckily without bruising himself. I do not know how the cousin got away – there sure was an inquest. Perhaps his peccadillo was forgiven after 45 years of loyal service, many of which were spent shoving coal into the boiler of the old steam engines.

1 large rabbit (it will almost certainly
  be farmed)
plain flour, for dusting
4 tablespoons olive oil
1 tablespoon butter
1 onion, peeled and chopped
1 carrot, peeled and chopped
1 stick celery, chopped
a small bunch of sage and rosemary,
  tied together
5 slices pancetta, roughly chopped
salt and pepper
50 white wine
1 x 440 g can peeled tomatoes,
  crushed
20 kalamata olives
olive oil
1 quantity Polenta (see page 112)

Chop the rabbit into manageable pieces or ask the butcher to do it for you. Dust the pieces lightly in flour. Heat 2 tablespoons of the oil in a large heavy-based saucepan (a cast-iron pot is perfect for this dish), and fry the rabbit pieces on all sides until they colour a nice golden brown Remove the rabbit from the pan and set aside.

Heat the butter and the rest of the oil in the same pan and fry the onion, carrot and celery until they soften. Add the herbs and pancetta, and return the rabbit to the pan. Season with salt and pepper and pour on the wine. Simmer until the wine has evaporated, then add the tomatoes and olives. Simmer with the lid askew for up to an hour, or as long as it takes for the rabbit to cook to a lovely soft consistency and for the sauce to reduce and the flavours intensify. Make the polenta following the recipe on page 112. When ready to serve, mound the polenta onto a big serving platter and surround with the rabbit and its sauce.

polenta biscotti
makes 25–30

There cannot be a polenta chapter without polenta biscotti, also called zaletti, meaning 'the yellow ones'. I particularly like them because they contain sultanas, which are the specialty product from where I live.

120 g unsalted butter
90 g caster sugar
1 egg
150 plain flour
120 g fine yellow semolina flour
2 tablespoons polenta
1 teaspoon baking powder
90 g sultanas, soaked in brandy
  and drained

Cream the butter and sugar in a mixing bowl until pale. Add the egg. Sift together the flour, semolina flour, polenta and baking powder. Fold into the butter mixture then stir in the drained sultanas. Wrap the dough in clingfilm and chill for 2 hours before use.

Preheat the oven to 180°C and grease or line a baking tray with non-stick baking paper.

To shape the biscuits, lightly knead the chilled dough and roll into long sausages of 2–2.5 cm diameter and cut into 2 cm discs. Press the discs lightly onto the baking tray – these biscuits need not be uniform in size. Bake for 15 minutes or until golden.

Loretta Sartori, who contributed the dessert recipes to my previous book, loves polenta because her parents, like me, are from the Veneto. She says that this cake will surprise not only with the resulting colour, but with its flavour and texture.

75 g plain flour

35 g polenta

50 g fine yellow semolina flour

1 teaspoon baking powder

60 g almond meal

125 g unsalted butter

140 caster sugar

4 egg yolks

2 eggs

60 g sultanas

50 g fine yellow semolina flour, extra

caster sugar, extra

amore di polenta | polenta cake | makes 1 x 20 cm cake

Preheat the oven to 170°C. Butter and flour a 20 cm round cake tin.

Sift the flour, polenta, semolina flour, baking powder and almond meal together. Cream the butter and sugar until light and fluffy. Gradually add the egg yolks and beat until incorporated. Add the whole eggs, one at the time, and continue beating until the mixture is a pale yellow.

Fold the sifted ingredients into the batter until just combined. Add the sultanas. Pour into the prepared tin and smooth the surface. Sprinkle over the extra semolina and caster sugar.

Bake for 40 minutes until the surface is golden and a skewer inserted into the centre comes out clean.

rice and rice soups

If polenta represents the rustic, the hearty and the filling, risotto, also originating in the north of Italy, represents sophistication and special occasions. Rice is almost universal, especially in combination with vegetables. When it comes to rice, the main point of difference between Italian cooking and other cuisine is risotto, for there is no other gastronomy where rice is elevated to royal status rather than being an accompaniment. In my restaurant I have witnessed many Asian diners – otherwise very responsive to pasta – leave risotto on the plate with a mixture of curiosity and less than concealed contempt. I figure that the type of rice used for risotto mustn't please, nor the manner in which it is cooked.

For the Italians, however, risotto is very desirable – creamy, velvety, rich or light – and it is a test of the host's ability in the kitchen. Furthermore, there are different risotto styles, depending on personal taste, region, ingredient and so on. Clearly, a risotto next to a braised meat like ossobuco cannot be too soupy. Conversely, an asparagus risotto should be, at least for me, a little runny – and that is a matter of personal taste, although you are likely to find a lot of Venetians agreeing with me.

The Venetian playwright Carlo Goldoni, whose work so cleverly captures the charming and decadent mood of Venice just before she was raped by the French invaders, made one of his characters criticise the Florentines because they allow their risotto to overcook and to double in volume. What he was saying, even then, is that risotto cannot be soft. Risotto rice is all about texture, a quality that makes it completely different from Asian or Indian rice. Again, people in my restaurant have complained about runny risotto, so much so that I now serve it less frequently. I am despondent to see risotto become another bastardised Italian dish. Asserting freedom of approach to culinary matters is one thing; bad taste and insensitivity is another. This seemingly banal dish is transformed into something sublime only when it is cooked with respect and with exceptional quality ingredients. Otherwise, forget it.

So, at the risk of repeating myself, a good risotto requires an exceptional chicken stock, a golden one full of flavour (see page 79). Over the years I have been guest chef at umpteen restaurants, which invariably use the same 'alla francese' stocks to make risotto. These over-reduced concoctions certainly have a place in the kitchen, but not near risotto. To my horror, I have also been in restaurant kitchens where they use chicken cubes and chicken booster to make risotto – goodness knows why, when a good stock is so simple to make. So, the secret to good risotto is a good stock, simple ingredients, and cooking it just right. Try it with the following recipes.

Certain dishes are at their best when made with fresh ingredients and this is one of them. I recommend using fresh rather than frozen scallops, and these are nearly always available in Australia. Ideally, you also need a couple of fresh herbs like chives and chervil; if not available, just use flat-leaf parsley. You must use a delicate stock for this dish.

24 fresh scallops

2 tablespoons butter

2 tablespoons olive oil

1 large onion, finely chopped

1/2 clove garlic, finely chopped

4 tablespoons diced zucchini

200 g Italian risotto rice

50 ml dry white wine

2 litres fish stock, simmering

salt and pepper

1 tablespoon chopped fresh chives

2 tablespoons chopped fresh chervil (optional)

a few drops of lemon juice

1 tablespoon butter

risotto with scallops and herbs | serves 4

Chop 8 of the scallops and keep the remaining 16 whole to add near the end of the cooking time.
Heat the butter and oil in a heavy-based pan and cook the onions and garlic until soft. Add the chopped scallops, zucchini and rice. Stir well, then add the wine. Toast the rice by frying it until it has absorbed all the wine and fat.
After a minute or so, begin to add the hot stock, a ladleful at a time, stirring constantly between addition until the stock is absorbed. Cook for 15–20 minutes, or until the rice is cooked, but each grain is still slightly firm in the centre. Taste and adjust for salt and pepper. Towards the end of the cooking time, add the whole scallops. Cook for a few minutes, then stir in the fresh herbs and the lemon juice. Remove from the heat and stir in the butter. Cover for few moments, then serve.

Asparagus can vary a lot in quality. Find them green and firm, or reject them and complain. The price is often too high, and the farmers don't get to see much of that money at all. If the prices in supermarkets were lower the farmers would sell a lot more produce and the public would be happier and better educated in food matters.

When you trim the asparagus, keep the hard woody stalks: you can cook them in a little water to extract that special asparagus flavour for use in stocks and soups.

40 g butter
40 ml olive oil
1 small brown onion, peeled and
 finely diced
400 g asparagus, trimmed and cut into
 small pieces (reserve the spears)
200 g Italian risotto rice
50 ml white wine
2 litres Golden Chicken Stock (see
 page 79), kept simmering
salt and pepper
1 tablespoon butter
parmesan to taste

Heat the butter and oil in a heavy-based pan and cook the onion until soft. Add the asparagus pieces (except the spears) and cook a little longer. Add the rice and the wine and 'toast' the rice by frying it until it has absorbed all the wine and the fat. After a minute or so, begin to add the hot stock, a ladleful at a time, stirring constantly. As the risotto is cooking, be careful not to drown the rice or allow it to become too dry. Cook for 15–20 minutes, or until the rice is cooked, but with each grain still slightly firm in the centre. Taste for salt and pepper – if you are using a well-made, good-quality stock you will need very little extra salt.

Towards the end of the cooking time, add the asparagus spears. This will give the risotto a better, brighter look. Remove from the heat and stir in the butter and a generous amount of cheese. Cover for 2 minutes to allow the butter and cheese to melt into the rice, then serve straightaway.

risotto with prawns and peas
serves 4

A lovely creamy risotto full of chunks of prawns and explosions of sweet peas. If you cannot get hold of fresh small peas, omit them and replace with finely diced zucchini or asparagus.

2 tablespoons butter
3 tablespoons olive oil
1 small brown onion, peeled and finely chopped
1 clove garlic, finely chopped
200 g Italian risotto rice
50 ml wine
2 litres light fish or chicken or vegetable stock
salt and pepper
12 medium-sized green prawns (if using whole prawns, remove the heads and shells and add to the stock for extra flavour)
300 g fresh peas, shelled
1 tablespoon butter
fresh chopped flat-leaf parsley
a squeeze of lemon
freshly ground black pepper (optional)

Heat the butter and 2 tablespoons oil in a heavy-based pan and cook the onion and garlic until soft. Add the rice and toast it by frying until it has absorbed all the flavours. Add the wine and simmer until it evaporates. After a minute or so, begin to add the hot stock, a ladleful at a time, stirring constantly between each addition.

Cook for 15–20 minutes, or until the rice is cooked, but each grain is still slightly firm in the centre. Taste and adjust for salt and pepper.
Meanwhile, cut the prawns into 2 cm chunks. Heat the remaining tablespoon of oil in a non-stick frying pan and briefly sear the prawns until they colour. Season with salt and pepper.
Five minutes before the end of cooking time, add the fresh peas to the risotto (so they maintain their lovely bright green colour). When the risotto is ready, stir in the prawns. Remove from the heat and stir in the butter and cover for few moments. Just before serving, add the parsley, lemon juice and, if you like, freshly ground black pepper.

Note: You can make a lovely flavoured oil with the heads and shells of shellfish such as prawns and yabbies. Simply place them on a baking tray and bake dry in a moderate oven until the shells are brittle and coloured. Tip them into a saucepan with half a head of garlic (cut crosswise) and cover with olive oil. Simmer very slowly, on the lowest heat you can achieve, for 2–3 hours, or until the crustacean flavour has really developed. This is a lovely oil to drizzle over seafood pasta and risotto, or even over simple grilled prawns. The oil will keep for a few weeks in a cool, dark cupboard.

riso in a broth
serves 4

Riso in brodo is one of the simplest and most delicious soups from northern Italy. It is a homely dish based on the principle of using good chicken stock, good rice and good cheese. When we talk about the simplicity of Italian cooking – vera cucina – this is it.

1.5 litres Golden Chicken Stock (see page 79)
200 g Italian soup rice
Parmigiano Reggiano, to taste

Bring the stock to the boil, add the rice and cook until al dente soft. Stir in the cheese to taste. If you have any chicken meat, dice it coarsely and add to the broth. I particularly like pieces of chicken livers.

rice with milk
Rice can also be cooked in milk instead of stock. It is a quirky taste, which is both slightly sweet and savoury. I guess it used to be regarded as nutritious food for children – I remember it from kinder days with the nuns! A pinch of salt is absolutely necessary to balance the sweetness of the milk.

This is a rice soup, rather than a risotto, as it does not need to be stirred. Simply add good chicken stock or a vegetable stock to the chosen base and then add your rice. A rice soup should be silky, healing and totally satisfying, like some of the Vietnamese or other Asian soups that we have become accustomed to.

2 tablespoons butter
2 tablespoons olive oil
1 small brown onion, peeled and finely chopped
1 medium-sized potato, peeled and very thinly sliced
2 litres hot Golden Chicken Stock (see page 79)
200 g Italian rice
300 g fresh asparagus, trimmed and cut into 1 cm pieces
salt and pepper
freshly grated parmesan, to taste

asparagus and rice soup | serves 4–6

Heat the butter and oil in a heavy-based pan and cook the onion and potato until soft. Add the hot stock and bring to the boil. Add the rice and lower the heat and simmer until the rice is soft. Just before the rice is ready, add the asparagus. This will keep some of the bright green colour. Season to taste and serve with freshly grated cheese to taste.

verdure

vegetables

vegetables

play a fundamental role in any cooking, but they have a special place in Italian cuisine because so much of it is based on rustic dishes developed at the time when there was a peasant culture. Where there was little money for beef and fish, vegetables provided a healthy alternative. A beautiful slice of eggplant, simply fried in olive oil, is for me as good as a steak.

I am a big fan of soft sformati, which are a kind of Italian custard made with a béchamel (white) sauce. Almost any vegetable can be turned into a sformato: mushrooms, zucchini, capsicum, eggplant – you name it. They are vegetarian and can be served cold as a starter or as a main course accompaniment. They save my life whenever vegetarians are in for dinner.

Porcini are Italian dried mushrooms. They are expensive, but you only need to use a few. You could also use porcini oil, which has some merit if not allowed to get too old and oxidised. A few drops can increase flavour.

100 g dried porcini mushrooms

200 g cultivated mushrooms

2 tablespoons butter

2 tablespoons olive oil

250 ml (⅛ quantity) Béchamel Sauce (see page 94), not too liquid

1 egg, lightly beaten

1/2 cup grated parmesan

salt and pepper

sformato of porcini | serves 6

Soak the porcini mushrooms in twice their volume of warm water for about 10 minutes to reconstitute them. Squeeze dry and combine with the cultivated mushrooms.

Heat the butter and oil in a frying pan and sauté the mushrooms. Cook until the liquid has reduced and then purée in a food processor.

Preheat the oven to 160°C.

Mix the mushrooms with the béchamel sauce, egg and parmesan, and season with salt and pepper.

Mix well and pour into 6 lightly greased plastic dariole moulds (which are available from many supermarkets) or ceramic soufflé ramekins. Fold a tea towel and place in the bottom of a deep baking tray. Arrange the dariole moulds in the tray and pour in enough warm water to come halfway up the sides of the moulds. Bake in the oven for about 35 minutes, or until set. The sformato should be fairly firm to the touch.

stuffed zucchini flowers
serves 4

Zucchini flowers are available during the season at specialist greengrocers, and you can grow them at home too. The flowers have little flavour, but when stuffed with cheese or anchovies, dipped in a light batter and deep-fried, they become the ultimate fast food.

This is not a fancy restaurant batter; it is thick and tasty. My children like it because the cooked flowers can be put into a sandwich for school lunch. Other children always want a taste of this mysterious food.

12 zucchini flowers
vegetable oil, for shallow-frying
olive oil, for shallow-frying
batter
180 g plain flour
2 eggs
40 g grated grana
1 clove garlic, chopped
a pinch of chopped flat-leaf parsley
water

Check the zucchini flowers to make sure they are quite clean – but it is best not to wash them. Pinch out the stamens and the little green bits around the base of the flower. If stuffing them, push in an anchovy fillet or a spoonful of seasoned ricotta mixed with a beaten egg.

Mix the batter ingredients together, adding enough water to make a soft consistency that will stick to the flowers without dripping off too quickly. Shallow-fry the zucchini in 2 cm of a vegetable and olive oil mixture. It will take about 1 minute on each side. Remove from the oil with a slotted spoon and drain on kitchen paper.

zucchini tart
serves 8

pastry
250 g plain flour
a pinch of salt
150 g unsalted butter, cubed
100 ml water, or enough to
    make a dough
filling
2 tablespoons butter
4–5 zucchini, cut into 3 mm slices
2 eggs, lightly beaten
100 ml cream
80 g parmesan, grated
1 egg white

To make the Pastry, put the flour, salt and butter in a food processor and pulse until the mixture resembles breadcrumbs. Add the water gradually, until the mixture just comes together to form a dough. Finish mixing it lightly with your hands and form into a round. Wrap the pastry in clingfilm and leave it to rest for an hour at room temperature.

Lightly grease a 23 cm tart tin. Roll out the pastry on a lightly floured work surface and use to line the prepared tin. Leave the edges overhanging. Transfer the pastry shell to the fridge and rest for an hour.

Preheat the oven to 150°C. Line the chilled tart shell with baking paper and fill with baking beans. Cook for 45 minutes, then remove from the oven and trim the edges neatly. Remove the beans and prick the bottom of the tart shell with a fork. Return the shell to the oven to dry for at least another 45 minutes.

To make the Filling, melt the butter in a large frying pan and sauté the zucchini until lightly browned all over.

In a mixing bowl, combine the eggs with the cream and parmesan. Lightly brush the base of the prepared pastry shell with egg white, then fill neatly with the zucchini slices. Pour the egg mixture into the tart, allowing it to seep in between the layers. Return to the oven and bake for 20 minutes, or until the filling has set. Serve with a salad.

zucchini chips

Hardly a recipe; more of an idea. Slice zucchini into rounds about 3–4 mm thick, roll them in flour and deep-fry in very hot oil. And there you have it: zucchini chips.

When I was little couldn't get enough of them. All kids like salty fried food, but as an adult I find them very pleasant with a glass of white wine or served with fish fillets instead of potato chips.

eggplant slice with mozzarella

This is truly an easy dish and an absolute favourite with my children. Serve as part of an antipasto selection or with a salad as a good vegetarian option. I have not given quantities; this is more a method than a recipe. The dish is best made with buffalo mozzarella.

olive oil, for frying
eggplant, cut into 2 cm slices
grated Grana Padano
salt and pepper
Italian tomato sauce
fresh basil leaves
fresh mozzarella

Preheat the oven to 180°C.
Heat the oil in a large pan and fry the eggplant until golden brown on both sides. Remove from the pan and drain well on absorbent paper. Arrange the slices in a baking dish, sprinkle with cheese and season lightly with salt and pepper. Spoon a little tomato sauce on each slice and top with a basil leaf. Cover with mozzarella and bake for 5 minutes, or until the mozzarella has melted. The eggplant should look like mini pizzas.

eggplant melanzane 'boiled and baked'
serves 4

A typical example of cucina povera, or cuisine of the poor, which is essentially the spirit of regional cooking. The eggplant are boiled, fried and baked, and, while seemingly fussy, they are not. They taste really good, and are well worth the effort.

4 medium-sized eggplant
2 cloves garlic, finely chopped
1 cup breadcrumbs
2 eggs
flat-leaf parsley or basil, finely chopped
150 g grated pecorino or Grana
    Padano, plus some extra
olive oil, for frying
400 ml Tomato Sauce (see page 153)
salt and pepper, to taste

Cut the eggplant lengthwise into 4 or more segments. The idea here is that when they are boiled and most of their flesh is scooped out, you must be left with enough skin to form a small boat that will accommodate the filling. Boil the eggplant segments in plenty of boiling salted water until they are reasonably soft. Lift out of the water and leave to rest on a cloth to the absorb the excess water.

When cold, use a spoon to scoop out the flesh, leaving at least 5 cm still on the skin. Mash the flesh and let it rest in a colander so that excess water can drain away. When drained stir in the garlic, breadcrumbs, eggs, parsley and cheese. The mixture must not be too wet. Spoon this mixture back into the eggplant 'shells' and shape them a bit. Preheat the oven to 180°C. Heat a little olive oil in a pan and begin to fry the 'shells' on the bottoms only. This ensures that the bottom part of the eggplant shell is crisp and cooked through. Remove from the pan and leave to rest on absorbent paper. Place in a baking dish and cover generously with tomato sauce. Sprinkle with the extra cheese and bake for 10 minutes or more until the sauce has blended with the eggplant. This dish is best eaten the day after, either reheated or cold.

From the traditional to the modern end of the Italian food spectrum. The tomatoes must be perfect – ripe and red and free of water. There is nothing to the rest of it, really, but it looks sensational. Recipe quantities will have to be adjusted depending on the size of the terrine mould you use, as well as the size, quality and substance of the tomatoes.

In the restaurant we have served this terrine with a simple rocket salad and quickly seared tuna, cut into neat slices. Otherwise it is lovely as it is, with a good bruschetta or some buffalo mozzarella on the side.

The quantities given are enough for 2 when made in a large ramekin.

olive oil, for frying
1 eggplant, peeled and cut into 5 mm slices
6 ripe red tomatoes, peeled, halved and seeded
5 basil leaves
salt
1 leaf gelatine
20 ml vegetable stock, warm

eggplant and tomato terrine | serves 2

Heat the olive oil in a heavy-based pan and fry the eggplant on both sides until lightly golden. Remove from the pan and drain on kitchen paper.

Arrange the tomatoes on kitchen paper for an hour or so to drain away as much moisture as possible. Line a terrine mould up the sides with the eggplant. Next, fill the mould with layers of tomato and basil leaves, salting each layer lightly as you go. When you reach the top of the mould, dissolve the gelatine in the warm stock and pour over the tomatoes. Cover with more slices of eggplant. Weight the terrine and refrigerate for a few hours. Cut into slices to serve.

broad bean stew
serves 6

Broad beans in season are a great treat. Stewed in a rich tomato sauce, they make a complete meal.

2 tablespoons olive oil
1 brown onion, finely chopped
4 cloves garlic, finely chopped
400 g shelled fresh broad beans
2 cups rich tomato sauce
1 cup Golden Chicken Stock (see page 79)
a piece of prosciutto skin or a few pieces of pancetta (optional)
salt and pepper

Heat the olive oil in a pan and sauté the onion and garlic until they soften and colour. Add the beans and stir well. Pour on the tomato sauce and stock. Add the prosciutto skin, if using, and season. Simmer on a low heat for around 20 minutes with the lid slightly askew, until the beans are tender.

broad beans
with cheese

A much celebrated treat is broad beans eaten with pecorino. Pecorino is cheese made with sheep's milk, so it has a rather strong and salty flavour. The fresh beans, by contrast, are tender and delicate. A bowl of good olive oil and some salt flakes provide extra flavour.

This is a theatrical dish. Present the individual components in rustic dishes in the centre of the table for diners to help themselves. The idea is for each person to shell their own beans, dip them into the oil and eat with the cheese. It goes without saying that a glass of light red wine is also very desirable. A great deal of Italian food is eaten in this way, where the food itself and the very act of eating it becomes something of a seasonal celebration. And it goes to show that you don't have to go to Tuscany to discover traditions – you can make them part of your own daily life.

roasted tomatoes with olives
serves 6

Another wonderful way of eating tomatoes is to roast them. Take them on a picnic, serve them as an antipasto or as a side dish with all sorts of meat or poultry dishes. To make roasted tomatoes a bit more interesting, add a few capers, olives and anchovies as you roast them.

12 ripe Roma tomatoes, halved
12 anchovy fillets, halved
20 small black olives (Ligurian are ideal)
a spoonful of capers, well rinsed
extra-virgin olive oil
salt

Preheat the oven to 160°C. Arrange the tomatoes on a baking tray. Top each tomato with a piece of anchovy. Scatter on the olives and capers, and drizzle generously with olive oil. Sprinkle with a bit of salt – not too much as the other ingredients are salty – and roast for 45 minutes.

braised small onions
serves 4

A greatly underrated dish, often bypassed in favour of horrible pickled onions. The combination of sugar and vinegar makes this dish very appetising. Choose lovely baby onions and serve them as a tasty condiment with roast beef.

1 tablespoon butter
1 tablespoon olive oil
1 tablespoon brown sugar
20 baby onions, peeled
5 cloves garlic, peeled
a splash of balsamic vinegar
a handful of sultanas
salt

Melt the butter and olive oil in a small saucepan, then add the sugar, onions and garlic and cook gently until they brown. Splash in the balsamic vinegar, add the sultanas and salt, and cook until the onions are tender and the juices have reduced, about 30 minutes. If the onions dry out, add a dash of water or stock as you go.

spinach with cream and parmigiano
serves 4

Spinach is universally acclaimed and fundamental to Italian cooking. I am not fond of the so-called baby spinach. I like proper big bunches of the stuff, even though it is a chore to wash. In this dish, spinach is combined with parmesan and cream, and finished with a touch of nutmeg.

butter, for frying
4 bunches spinach, washed and trimmed
100 ml cream
100 g grated parmesan
salt
freshly grated nutmeg

Melt some butter in a large pan and cook the spinach until it wilts. Tip the spinach out into a colander, and leave to drain. Better still, squeeze dry. In the same saucepan, heat the cream with a little dollop of additional butter. Return the drained spinach to the pan and stir into the cream. Add the cheese and stir well to combine. Season lightly with salt and finish with a good grating of nutmeg. As this is rather a wet dish, serve in a small bowl rather than on a serving plate.

green bean and cherry tomato salad
serves 6

The sight of green beans in a bowl with cherry tomatoes, all drenched in the freshest olive oil, is a very happy one. This is a simple summer salad that can become almost a meal in itself when served with some crusty bread. It is also the perfect accompaniment to lamb chops, marinated in a little fresh rosemary.

500 g small green beans, trimmed
2 punnets cherry tomatoes (split the tomatoes in half if they are too big)
1 clove garlic, shaved on at the last minute
extra-virgin olive oil
salt flakes

Cook the beans in plenty of boiling water until just tender, drain well and plunge into cold water to cool. Place the beans in a large bowl with all the remaining ingredients and toss to combine.

baked fennel with star anise
serves 4

I am particularly fond of soft-baked fennel. This dish is perfect to accompany a pork roast, and is especially good with Slow Roasted Pork Belly (see page 194).

3 large fennel bulbs
3 pieces star anise
chicken stock, well seasoned

Preheat the oven to 180°C.
Trim the fennel bulbs and cut them in half lengthwise. Remove the hard core and cut into long slices. Blanch in hot water till they are soft. Pack the slices in a baking dish and scatter on the star anise. Pour on a little stock and cover with foil. Bake for 30 minutes, then remove the foil and bake until the surface turns crisp and brown.

avocado, orange and leaf salad
serves 4

Avocado and oranges are a wonderful combination. Where you grow oranges you can also grow avocados. Where I live, it is not uncommon to see an avocado plantation with citrus groves on either side. Some rocket, radicchio or frisée lettuce provides a nice bridge between the oranges and the avocado.

2 heads red radicchio
2 oranges
1 large ripe avocado
a handful of rocket
extra-virgin olive oil, to taste
a few drops of lemon juice
salt flakes

Select the better radicchio leaves and tear into bite-sized pieces. With a sharp knife, cut away the pith from the oranges and cut out segments between the membranes. To assemble, cut the avocado in half and peel. Dice the flesh. In a bowl, mix the rocket, avocado, orange and radicchio. Dress with oil, lemon juice and salt flakes.

You sometimes find calzone in pizza shops, although, as a rule, they seem to be on the menu more as an afterthought, and are not that good. Well-made calzone are delicious. All it takes is a pizza dough (see page 56) and interesting filling ingredients.

2 big bunches silverbeet, washed and drained
2 tablespoons olive oil
2 cloves garlic, finely chopped
1 small chilli, finely chopped, or to taste
salt and pepper
300 g Pizza Dough (see page 56)
5 slices prosciutto (optional)
a handful of grated cheese such as pecorino
1 egg, lightly beaten

calzone with silverbeet | serves 4

Slice the silverbeet, and separate the stalks from the leaves. Blanch the stalks in boiling water until tender. Briefly blanch the leaves. Drain and cool both stalks and leaves. Chop together, then squeeze firmly to extract any excess water. You should have a nice pile of soft silverbeet.
Heat the oil in a large frying pan and lightly fry the garlic and chilli. Add the silverbeet and toss in the oil. Season with salt and pepper to taste. Remove from the heat and cool.
Preheat the oven to 180°C.
Roll out the pizza dough to a sheet of around 4 mm thickness. Arrange the prosciutto across the bottom half of the pastry, if using, then top with the silverbeet and cheese. Bring the other half of the pastry up and over the filling. Brush the edges with a little egg and press to seal. Trim away any excess pastry. Pierce the surface with a fork and brush with a little more beaten egg. Transfer to a baking sheet and bake in the oven for 10 minutes until golden brown.

oranges & the sunraysia

Did you know that an orange with a Sunkist sticker is of Californian provenance? There is yet another, also from California, with the suggestive name of 'Dole', a term more likely to be pertinent to the condition of an Australian grower whose orange tree trunks have been – to quote a line from one of Les Murray's poems – 'globalised out of the ground'. I have nothing against free trade, God forbid, until I see my next-door neighbour bury his fruit. Then I put all reason aside, because it is my community that's under pressure, not some highly paid bureaucrat working on the GATT.

Putting aside international trade issues, which are complex, not least because free trade allows us to export citrus to other countries, the domestic demand of a nation approaching 20 million people should be strong enough to support our relatively small industry of about 600,000 tonnes annually. Judging by the sheer number of magazines, books, TV programs, videos and regular articles devoted to food, an outsider would be justified in thinking we are a nation obsessed with the pleasures of the table. In such a gastronomic heaven, it should not be difficult to flog – pardon the expression – a few more tonnes of mandarins each year. And yet this does not happen and our citrus growers, once a very fortunate group, are now a struggling lot.

One credible theory to explain the troubles of citrus is that it now has to compete with other fruits that are not just apples and bananas. There is a bit of everything out there all the time, partly due to imports of fruit that normally would be out of season, and fruit that are cleverly packaged, like fresh, sliced pineapple with the skin removed. Citrus, lacking in packaging and therefore in glamour, tends to be taken for granted; besides, it makes your hands sticky and messy.

Another theory – and this comes from the producers – is that the time it takes from the farm to the table is too long, the process is haphazard, the displays are poor and fruit rotation is not managed properly. These problems affect the quality of the product, and that in turn affects public opinion. Talking of displays, I would certainly like these to show, as is mandatory under the law, which is the imported fruit. Signage should be clearly legible and in a prominent position. A galling thing to producers, I'm reliably told, is the constant request from the distributors, who work with the supermarkets, for largish fruit. This drives down the price of smaller fruit, but when you buy it, you don't pay less for it. Yet consumers have indicated a preference for smaller oranges because they fit neatly into their squeezing devices. So, why is it that supermarkets demand larger fruit? Figure that out if you can.

Perhaps the sad reality is that Australia is not a place where fresh fruit is sought after. It is never served, for instance, after dinner other than as a fruit salad in poor man bistros. Chinese restaurants have been the exception, but even these have been criticised by food critics for insisting on fresh fruit after main course rather than offering contemporary desserts.

Fruit does not feature greatly in that Australian institution, the 'takeaway food' sector, and even less in that special place where collective approaches to food are in part determined: the school yard.

I am sure that those who appreciate citrus love it in all its dimensions and I invite them to explore it further in their cooking. Perhaps one of the most effective ways to use citrus is to introduce its skin, peeled or grated, into a variety of foods you haven't thought of. A little grated lemon, mixed with flat-leaf parsley and finely chopped garlic, makes gremolata, which is very effective sprinkled over long-braised dishes such as ossobuco or lamb shanks. You can also use it with a whole variety of fish dishes. Lemon is indispensable for a whole lot of Mediterranean dishes, especially when combined with olive oil, oregano, rosemary and other herbs. The dried skin of tangerines – but any orange would do – is very popular in Chinese cooking. Candied orange skins go into a variety of desserts and are available commercially. The juice of limes is indispensable in many Asian dishes – think of the Thai combination of palm sugar, fish sauce and lime juice. And let's not forget the lime that makes gin and tonic the drink for all occasions!

When the oranges are raging from June
onward and fennel bulbs are pushing their
way out of the winter-cold ground, it is
time for this wonderful Sicilian salad. It is
a refreshing dish, more of a stand-alone
than a side show. The sweet and sour
orange flavour blends beautifully with the
salty olives and fruity olive oil. Fennel
provides crunch and a refreshing anise
quality. I like to serve it as part of an
antipasto – perhaps with some prawns
or marinated fish.

6 navel oranges
1 large fennel bulb or 2 smaller ones
24 green olives
extra-virgin olive oil
salt flakes

orange, fennel and green olive salad | serves 6

Use a sharp knife to slice off both ends of the oranges. Peel each orange, then carefully cut away all the
pith. Cut the oranges into slices and arrange on a large serving platter.
Cut the fennel in half lengthwise, then cut each half into thin wedges and arrange on top of the orange
slices. Scatter on the olives. Drizzle with olive oil and sprinkle on salt to taste.

This sweet citrus salad is a joy to see and quite a taste sensation. I like to think of it as a base to which more elements can be added, such as pineapple or ice-cream, but with the contrasting elements of sweetness and chilli-heat, it is equally good just as it is.

3 oranges

2 pink grapefruit (or 1 pink and 1 standard grapefruit)

150 g caster sugar

juice of 1 orange

juice of 1 lemon

½ teaspoon finely chopped chilli

½ teaspoon finely chopped ginger

5 cm piece lemongrass stalk, split in half

sweet orange salad | serves 4

Use a sharp knife to peel the oranges and grapefruit. Carefully slice away all the pith and cut into manageable slices – they shouldn't be too thin.

Place the sugar in a small saucepan with enough water to just cover. Bring to a boil, then simmer until it forms a light blond syrup. Remove from the heat and add the orange and lemon juices. Be careful that it doesn't spatter and burn you. The sugar will harden, but will dissolve again as you stir. When the syrup has cooled a little, add the chilli and ginger. Once it has cooled completely, add the lemongrass and leave the syrup to infuse.

Pour the cold syrup over the sliced fruit and leave to marinate for a few hours in the fridge. Serve chilled or at room temperature, as preferred.

Globe artichokes are another vegetable that Italians love; their nutty, earthy taste is always welcome at the dinner table. Artichokes are very versatile and may be boiled, braised, grilled or deep-fried. Artichokes preserved in oil make a delicious addition to an antipasto selection or to a pizza topping.

This recipe is easy to make. Just make sure that you choose artichokes that are fresh and firm, and not limp, oxidised or yellow. Artichokes should be a vivid green, and may have streaks of deep purple on the leaves. One variety I particularly like has pointed leaves that can be a bit prickly at the tips. Late in the season rogue farmers may send artichokes to market with a central 'choke' – a horrible hairy fluff that must be discarded – which means that the fruit is mature and going to flower. The only edible part is the base – and the artichokes should be given to you free of charge!

6 large artichokes

100 ml olive oil

3 cloves garlic, chopped

3 anchovies (optional)

a splash of white wine

1 bunch flat-leaf parsley, stalks and leaves, chopped

1 litre Golden Chicken Stock (see page 79)

salt

braised artichokes | serves 6 as an accompaniment

Remove the tough outer leaves from the artichokes and lob off the top third. Peel the stalks, leaving about 4 cm attached to the fruit. Don't discard all the stalks, though – any tender parts can also be peeled and cooked.

Heat the oil in a large non-reactive saucepan and add the garlic, anchovies and artichokes and a splash of white wine. After a few moments add the parsley, and then the stock. The artichokes should be completely covered. Cover the pan and simmer for 20 minutes. Then turn them over in the liquid. Cook for another 10–15 minutes. By the end of the cooking time, most of the liquid should have evaporated. Season to taste.

When you eat these artichokes you are allowed to chew and suck on the leaves!

8 soft-boiled eggs, not too hard

finely chopped flat-leaf parsley

a drizzle of strong extra-virgin olive oil

grated grana, to taste

tomato sauce

1½ tablespoons good olive oil

1 brown onion, peeled and chopped

1 clove garlic, chopped

1 x 400 g tin Italian tomatoes or 400 g ripe fresh Roma tomatoes, chopped

salt and pepper

a handful of basil or flat-leaf parsley

eggs braised in tomato | serves 4

To make the Tomato Sauce, heat the olive oil in a pan and sauté the onion and garlic until they soften and colour lightly. Add the tomatoes and cook for around 30 minutes. Taste, and season with salt and pepper. Towards the end of the cooking time add the basil.

Peel the eggs and cut them in half lengthwise. Heat the tomato sauce in a smallish casserole or saucepan. Arrange the eggs in the sauce, sunny-side up, and simmer gently until the eggs have warmed through and the flavours have developed. Sprinkle with fresh parsley, a drizzle of strong extra-virgin olive oil and grated grana. Serve with toast.

Comfort food at its best! You need a rich tomato sauce as a base in which you cook the thinly sliced zucchini. You then crack some eggs straight into the sauce and poach gently. Serve with freshly cracked black pepper and a piece of chunky toasted bread.

1 quantity Tomato Sauce (see page 153)
400 g zucchini, thinly sliced
salt and pepper
4 eggs
several thin slices provolone cheese (optional)
freshly cracked black pepper

eggs and 'wet' zucchini | serves 4

Heat the tomato sauce in a smallish casserole or saucepan. Add the zucchini, and simmer gently until the water they release has reduced. Season with salt and pepper, then crack the eggs straight into the sauce and poach them to your preferred consistency. Towards the end of the cooking time, top with the provolone cheese slices (if using) and serve with plenty of black pepper.

penne pasta baked with tomatoes
serves 4–5

tomato sauce and ricotta
serves 4

An ideal dish to make at the height of summer when tomatoes are abundant, ripe and juicy. Peel a couple of kilograms of tomatoes (plunge them in boiling water first, to make this easier), then slice. Meanwhile, toss 400 g of raw penne in 100 ml olive oil and leave them for 2 hours to absorb as much oil as possible.

Layer the bottom of a baking dish with slices of tomato followed by a layer of pasta. Repeat until all the pasta and tomatoes have been used. Season with salt and pepper as you go. Cover with aluminium foil and bake in a preheated 180°C oven for 25 minutes.

The result should be a lovely, soft and juicy dish. If too wet, return to the oven for a little longer. As you serve, scatter on a generous handful of torn basil leaves and plenty of freshly grated parmesan (or bocconcini or buffalo mozzarella). A slug of your best olive oil would also be good. As you can tell, there are many variables to this dish. And it is well worth making over and over again until you perfect it.

The idea is to make a good fresh tomato sauce using a base of slowly stewed onions that have been flavoured with chopped garlic and fresh ginger – use a teaspoon of each for every cup of onions. Add the tomatoes, then, while the sauce is simmering, add a few curry leaves, a pinch of chilli powder and salt. Meanwhile, cut the ricotta into 4 cm slices. Obviously you'll need one of the firmer styles of ricotta – and only buy as much as you need. Fry the ricotta in a little olive oil in a non-stick pan until golden brown. There is no need to dust them in flour before frying, and it doesn't matter if they break up a little as they cook. Gently lift the ricotta into the bubbling tomato sauce and cook for a few minutes.

This is delicious served with an Indian-style bread. If you like, top with a handful of fresh coriander leaves.

pesce

fish

fish

Even though they are a diminishing resource, Australia still enjoys quite a wide variety of fish and crustaceans. Fish farming will continue on a larger scale and although that can present some environmental problems, it is one way of satisfying the world demand for fish. Australia is an interesting continent when it comes to fish, because a huge variety of fish, molluscs and crustaceans is found here. It is possible to replicate most Mediterranean dishes without much effort. If you are lucky enough you can also catch a fish in many of our inland rivers and waterways. Although I have some misgivings about recreational angling, I admit it is hard to resist going fishing. One can always let the fish go – hard, but probably sensible. Italian cooking tends to combine fish with something else, for instance tomato, olives, polenta, pasta or rice. Garlic and parsley also play a major role. It is fantastic to be able to play with all these ingredients! Usually the fresh cooking method is short and fuss free, so that the fish is shown off to its best advantage.

This is not really a fish soup, but then there is no exact translation for guazzetto, which is a rather wet tomato-based fish dish. In this recipe the freshness of the fish will determine the outcome. A particular sensibility to fish is needed to understand how to bring it all together without overcooking.

20 clams or pipis, cleaned

20 mussels, cleaned and debearded

2 medium-sized calamari, cut into squares

4 large prawns, unshelled

4 scampi or Moreton Bay bugs (or add more prawns)

2 white fish fillets (don't use salmon or other oily fish), cut into bite-sized pieces

olive oil

a generous slug of white wine

400 ml Tomato Sauce (see page 153)

5 fresh, ripe tomatoes, peeled and diced

a touch of chopped chilli

freshly chopped flat-leaf parsley

fish guazzetto, almost a soup | serves 4

Clean and prepare the seafood.

Heat the olive oil in a large heavy-based saucepan. Add the clams and white wine and steam until they open. Strain off the liquor to remove any sand and set the clams aside. Repeat, to open the mussels. Wipe the pan clean and heat a little more oil. Quickly sear the prawns until they turn pink. Set aside while you repeat with the scampi and calamari. Finally, sear the fish fillets on both sides and set aside with the other seafood.

Add the tomato sauce to the pan and bring to the boil. Add the fresh tomatoes and chilli. Carefully return the seafood to the pan, starting with the fish, then the prawns, scampi, calamari, mussels and clams. Add the strained liquor, avoiding any sand. If the dish is very thick you may need to add a little fish stock or water to thin slightly. Simmer for a few minutes until the flavours have melded. Sprinkle with fresh parsley and serve with grilled bread that has been rubbed with a little garlic and good olive oil.

More often than not, calamari is served in some deep-fried form. In this dish it is stuffed and slowly braised in a rich tomato sauce. One of the key stuffing ingredients is sultanas, which add a delicious and unexpected sweet dimension.

Back in the 1930s in my home-town, Mildura, a man by the name of De Garis undertook a massive marketing campaign to promote locally grown sultanas. There were amazing cash prizes and other incentives, and for a while Australia became sultana crazy! Sadly, nowadays sultanas have become almost overlooked. They pop up in the odd fruit bun or breakfast cereal, but these tend to be cheaper imports from countries like Turkey. When it comes to quality and flavour, however, there is nothing to match the Mildura 'five-crown' sultana.

4 medium-sized calamari

extra-virgin olive oil

a splash of white wine

salt and pepper

300 g cooked Italian rice

2 tablespoons dried sultanas, plumped up in a bit of weak tea and drained

2 tablespoons chopped fennel tips (use wild fennel if you can find it)

1 tablespoon salted capers, rinsed

1 teaspoon grated lemon or orange zest

2 eggs

4 tablespoons fresh breadcrumbs

a sprinkle of grated pecorino

400 ml Tomato Sauce (see page 153)

2 fresh tomatoes, skinned and diced

calamari filled with sultanas and rice | serves 4

Prepare the calamari by removing the heads, tentacles and wings. Keep the calamari tubes to one side and discard the heads. Finely chop the tentacles and wings.

Heat a little olive oil in a frying pan and sear the chopped calamari quickly with a splash of wine and season with salt and pepper.

In a mixing bowl, combine the cooked calamari with the rice, sultanas, fennel, capers, zest, eggs, breadcrumbs and cheese. Mix well to form a soft stuffing. Add more seasoning and cook a little of the mixture to taste if you feel unsure about the seasoning. Fill each calamari tube with stuffing, leaving a little space at the open end for the stuffing to expand. Secure the ends with toothpicks.

Heat the tomato sauce in a medium-sized saucepan. Add the stuffed calamari and cook gently until tender, 30–40 minutes. Towards the end of the cooking time add the tomatoes to give texture and freshness to the sauce. The calamari themselves do not have great flavour; it is the combination of rich tomato sauce and tasty stuffing that makes the finished dish interesting.

squid with peas and tomatoes
serves 6

There are several ways of cooking this dish – and it can also be made 'in bianco' (that is, without tomatoes). If you do decide to cook it in bianco, take even more care to select absolutely spanking-fresh squid. And I do mean squid, rather than calamari, octopus or cuttlefish. Squid is readily available and quite cheap, and has a unique colour, texture and flavour.

60 ml olive oil
1 onion, peeled and finely chopped
3 cloves garlic, peeled and finely
   chopped
1 kg fresh squid, cleaned and
   chopped into small pieces
a splash of white wine
a pinch of dried chilli flakes
salt and pepper
200 g peas (frozen works as well)
400 g peeled tomatoes
1 small bunch flat-leaf parsley
   (leaves only)

Heat the oil in a large pan and cook the onion and garlic until soft. Add the squid, wine, chilli flakes and season to taste with salt and pepper. Add the peas and tomatoes. Cook for 40 minutes or more, until the squid is tender. Check for seasoning, and toss in the parsley leaves just before serving.

mussels with fresh herbs
serves 4

Mussels are cheap and readily available all year round. Many Australians still regard them as bait for fish, but for me they a source of fun as well as being delicious. Dunking crusty bread into mussels and their sauce is one of the great pleasures of the communal table.
Many Mediterranean seafood dishes tend to be tomato-based, and mussels are no different. Try them without tomatoes for a change, or only add a couple of diced tomatoes to the recipe that follows.

olive oil
3 cloves garlic, coarsely chopped
2 kg fresh mussels
a splash of white wine
1 bunch fresh flat-leaf parsley
grated zest of ½ lemon
chopped chilli, to taste

You may have to cook this dish in batches if your heat source isn't strong. Heat some oil in a large pan, add the garlic, mussels, wine, followed by all the other ingredients.
Place a lid on the pan and cook until all the mussels have opened; this only takes a couple of minutes.
You can also add some fresh mint with the parsley.

crab in its shell

There are all kinds of crab available at different times of the year and from a diversity of Australian regions, but the most common, at least in Southern Australia, the blue swimmer crab, is outstanding for the sweetness of its meat and its cheap price – and it never lets you down. The uninitiated to the mysteries of another delicious crab, the mud crab, can choose between the risk of getting a real lemon for top dollars or heading for the nearest Chinese restaurant for a more reliable feed. I have persevered with all manner of crabs and found them, at times, wanting in terms of the ratio of price to meat content. However, when it comes to blue swimmers, I have rarely had a bad experience; if there was something wrong it was entirely attributable to the fishmonger. I must hasten to say that those pre-cooked ones that end up on seafood platters after doing time in the freezer can be fairly ordinary. But take a blue swimmer straight out of clean South Australian waters, plunge it in boiling water flavoured with a handful of herbs and after 5 minutes, or just enough time for the meat to set, you are bound to experience one of Australia's greatest delicacies.

These so-called blue swimmers are fished in the Spencer Gulf in South Australia by licensed fisher-men whose quota is capped to ensure the on-going viability of the industry. They are also seasonal in that fishing ceases during part of summer. Females tend to look green to brown in colour and are said to contain the better meat. I rarely see them as I believe fishermen do the 'right thing' and put them back.

There is much to be said for not fussing with things like crabs or yabbies: cook them simply, get into them, chew them, make a mess and enjoy. Blue swimmers can be savoured with a little extra-virgin olive oil, but not with lemon because, at least for me, lemon compromises the authenticity of their flavour, which is both sweet and nutty at the same time.

Cooked in tomato with extra-virgin olive oil, garlic, onions, celery and fennel and a touch of chilli, blue swimmers make the best spaghetti sauce you can taste. In this case cooking is not a five-minute job: it is a matter of patience and understanding when the fine balance between the tomato flavour and the crab flavour has been achieved. There is nothing more incomplete than a sauce where the tomato has not reduced to the right consistency and leaves a certain amount of liquid at the bottom of your spaghetti bowl. This is a party dish, a Sunday-lunch affair for people who are not afraid of getting their hands dirty.

There are other ways of enjoying this crab without much sucking and slurping and squirting of tomato sauce over one's shirt. Being such a delicate meat, it is very suitable as a starter for an elegant dinner party (does such a thing still exist?). Extract the meat and place it back in its shell – that's the basic idea. Crabmeat served in its shell is a dish I have enjoyed in the finest Chinese restaurants. I suspect that the meat is bound with egg before it is quickly gratinated or baked in the oven. I have never been game to ask for the recipe, fearing a refusal of the information or an insurmountable degree of technical difficulty.

But you cannot go wrong with crabs anyway, so give them a go.

A great way of retaining flavour and moisture in all fish and shellfish is to steam them. The crabs must be extremely fresh. Aromatic herbs add an appetising aroma and taste.

6 large blue swimmer crabs or more
4 cm fresh ginger, peeled and chopped
2 long red chillies, chopped
2 cloves garlic
a few small pieces of lemon peel
fresh coriander leaves
fresh flat-leaf parsley

steamed aromatic crab | serves 4–6

Turn the crab over so it rests on its shell. Remove the bottom flap, pull out and discard the 'dead man's fingers' and cut each crab in half. If they are large, cut into manageable pieces. Mix with all the aromatics in a bowl.

Bring a pot of water to the boil and arrange a steamer on top. Arrange half the crabs in a shallow bowl and place in the steamer basket. Cover and steam for 6 minutes, or until cooked. Carefully remove the bowl, taking care not to lose the tasty juices in the bottom. Repeat with the remaining crabs and serve straightaway. If you have a large steamer or use a wok, you can cook the crabs all at once.

An ideal dish for springtime, when snapper is readily available. Use a whole fish or a filleted side. Remember that whole fish will take longer to cook, so the timing is critical for the texture of the finished dish. I think the combination of olives and fennel is wonderful. It is important to blanch the fennel so it is partly cooked before you roast it. The type of baking dish you choose is also important: in my view an old aluminium tray works better than anything else.

1 x 1–2 kg whole snapper, gutted and cleaned

1–2 bulbs fennel, depending on size

extra-virgin olive oil

a few knobs of butter

a splash of white wine

salt and pepper

30 small black olives (Ligurian are ideal)

5 ripe tomatoes, peeled, seeded and finely diced

10 cloves garlic, lightly crushed, skin left on

roasted snapper with olives and fennel | serves 5

Preheat the oven to 180°C.

Rinse the snapper and pat dry. Bring a large pot of salted water to the boil. Clean the fennel bulbs and remove the outer leaves. Cut in half lengthwise and remove the hard inner core. Cut into wedges around 5 mm thick. Blanch in boiling water for a couple of minutes, then refresh in cold water to stop them cooking further.

Drizzle some olive oil in the base of a baking tray and scatter over the butter. Arrange the fennel in the tray and place the fish on top. Splash on the wine, season the fish with salt and pepper, and scatter on the olives, tomatoes and garlic.

Roast for 30 minutes, checking from time to time to ensure the vegetables and fish do not burn. Test the fish by inserting a sharp knife in the thickest part close to the bone to see if it is done. Return to the oven for a few more minutes if necessary. Squeeze the garlic out of its skin and eat with the fish. Serve with a fresh salad.

In *carpione* means marinated in vinegar and wine. This seemingly simple dish is excellent, especially when prepared using flathead. It makes a wonderful and unusual addition to an antipasto selection. Like the recipe for Sardines in Saor (see page 176), I suspect it was created before the advent of refrigeration, to preserve the fish for a few days.

1 kg flathead fillets, cut into smaller pieces, depending on size

plain flour, for dusting

olive oil, for frying

butter, for frying

5 medium-sized carrots, cut into 3 mm thick rounds

Golden Chicken Stock (see page 79) or water

300 ml dry white wine

300 ml good quality white vinegar

whole peppercorns

3 whole fresh bay leaves

salt and pepper

flathead in carpione | serves 6 or more

Dust the flathead pieces lightly in flour. Heat a little olive oil in a large frying pan and fry the fish on both sides until a light golden brown. Remove from the pan and drain on kitchen paper.

Heat a little more oil and some butter in the same pan and add the carrots. Sauté over a low heat.

Add a splash of stock or water and sauté slowly until the carrots are tender.

In a separate pan, bring the wine to the boil. Remove from the heat and leave to cool. When cold, stir in the vinegar.

Arrange some pieces of fish in a smallish, non-reactive dish and top with the carrots. Sprinkle on the peppercorns, tuck the bay leaves in among the fish pieces and season with salt and pepper as you go. Continue layering the fish and carrots until they are all used up. They should fit rather snugly. Pour the wine–vinegar mixture over the top. Cover and refrigerate for at least one day before serving.

sardines in saor
serves 6

Another old-fashioned dish from the days before refrigeration, when ways had to be found to preserve fish. Vinegar, being acid, is a strong preserving agent, and the Venetians invented a method of preserving sardines – the most abundant fish in the Adriatic Sea – in a vinegar-based marinade. They also like to incorporate sweet sultana grapes to balance the sourness of the vinegar. These were grown on the sunny islands of Greece – and many of the vineyards were owned by the Venetians themselves.

24 sardines
plain flour, for dusting
oil, for frying
4 medium-sized brown onions,
    thinly sliced
500 ml white vinegar
50 g sultanas
50 g pine nuts
salt and pepper

Scale the sardines and remove the heads, leaving the rest of the body whole. Dust lightly with flour.
Heat a good quantity of oil for frying in a large pan and fry the fish. When the fish are done, drain on absorbent paper. Discard the oil.
Heat a little fresh oil in a pan and gently fry the onions until they soften. Add the vinegar, then remove the pan from the heat and leave to cool.
Arrange a layer of sardines in a smallish non-reactive dish. Sprinkle on some sultanas and pine nuts and a good layer of onions. Season lightly with salt and pepper, and repeat until all the ingredients have been used. Pour on the vinegar, then cover and refrigerate for a couple of days to allow the flavours to develop and intensify.
They are nice on their own, or served as part of an antipasto selection.

stracciatella with crab meat
serves 4

8 blue swimmer crabs
1 litre fish stock or light chicken stock
4 eggs
salt and pepper

Steam the crabs for 5 minutes. You may have to steam them in two batches, depending on the size of your steamer. Leave them to cool, then pick all the meat from the shells and claws. Reserve until you are ready to eat.
Heat the stock in a large saucepan. Taste to ensure it is well seasoned, and adjust if necessary. In a separate bowl, beat the eggs together briskly. Season well with salt and pepper. Divide the crab meat between 4 serving bowls. Remove the hot stock from the heat and pour in the eggs in a slow steady stream, stirring all the while. They will quickly set in the heat. Pour the stracciatella into the serving bowls.

176

pollo e carne

poultry & meat

Australia is a meat paradise. There is everything one wants and more.

Beef and lamb are abundant in all sorts of cuts and from different kinds of animals. Australians are spoilt because prices here are still relatively cheap compared to other parts of our world. And what's more, immigration has brought in another set of cooking styles to complement the barbecue and the Sunday roast. Braising and slow-cooking of parts such as shanks and cheeks are relatively recent additions to the modern Australian repertoire.

On top of that, the quality of poultry has improved out of sight. Free-range chickens are readily available; duck, quail and pigeon are no longer regarded as weird things to eat. The public is offered a great number of choices out there, especially in the most advanced and sophisticated restaurants.

As for me, I remain very keen on offal, even though I get the distinct impression that I am not converting many followers. I came to offal simply because I was brought up on a farm and money was tight. The availability of meat was directly proportional to what we could grow by way of poultry and pork, but beef was out of reach. That's why, on a rare visit to the butcher, my father would return with such strange things as a calf's head, transported on the handlebars of his bike, or some tongue or shanks.

Many offal dishes are about enjoying texture. What may be fat to someone is sublime jelly to another, especially if dressed with a little salt and olive oil.

Lesser cuts are very delectable when poached or 'boiled'. Think of brisket, which is not offal, but when boiled, melts in the mouth and makes a great warm salad to be had with mustard sauce. The chapter on preserves features a recipe with ox tongue, which is poached. Ox tongue is great served with boiled spuds and a green sauce made with flat-leaf parsley.

Tripe, which I like serving with polenta, is best if cooked from raw. It requires long, slow cooking, as with any other 'casserole'-style dish. Tripe and oxtail, cooked for long enough without hurry and with a little care, produces a rich sauce. The addition of aromatics such as citrus rind improves the dish out of sight.

Roasted quail! How can one convey to those from a different gastronomic culture the sense of elation that fills me when I think of roasted quail?

The essential elements here are the pancetta and the small olives. They combine well with the wine to form a most appetising sauce.

8 quail

16 slices pancetta

a handful of sage leaves

olive oil

butter

80 ml white wine

a few sprigs of rosemary

24 small olives

8 cloves garlic, unpeeled and crushed

200 ml chicken stock

30 g butter

salt and pepper

roasted quail with small olives | serves 4

Preheat the oven to 180°C.

Remove the small wings from the quail (as they look unsightly). Roughly chop 8 slices of pancetta (reserve 8 whole slices for wrapping) and stuff into the quail with the sage. Tie the quail neatly and wrap each with a slice of pancetta.

Heat some olive oil and butter in a pan and sear the quail all over. Add a splash of the white wine and simmer for a few moments. Transfer the quail and pan juices to a baking tray and scatter on the rosemary sprigs, olives and garlic. Cook for 15 minutes until the quail is cooked pink. Remove from the oven and leave to rest in a warm place while you finish the sauce.

Heat the roasting juices, add the rest of the white wine and chicken stock and simmer until reduced. Whisk in the butter to form a nice glossy sauce. Taste and adjust the seasoning as necessary. Serve the quail on a mound of white polenta (see page 108) with the sauce and olives.

A small chicken is perfect for this recipe. It is such a simple dish that I am almost embarrassed to include it. And yet every time I cook it I am amazed by the result.

1 x 1.3 kg free-range chicken, cut into small pieces
extra-virgin olive oil
6 cloves garlic, peeled and left whole
50 ml white wine
a small sprig of rosemary
salt and pepper
a few small anchovies (optional)
1 tablespoon capers (optional)
2 tomatoes, skinned and diced (optional)

tender chicken with rosemary | serves 4

Prepare the chicken pieces and pat dry. Heat the oil in a non-stick casserole pan, add the whole garlic cloves and the chicken and brown evenly on a high heat. Add the wine and rosemary, and season with salt and pepper. If you are using the anchovies and capers, add them at this point.
Cover the pan, leaving the lid slightly askew. Simmer gently for around 35 minutes, adding a little stock or water if necessary. Towards the end of the cooking time, add the tomatoes if you desire a more juicy sauce. Serve the chicken with a simple green salad.

It is best to use duck maryland in this dish. There is no need to separate the thigh and leg, although you can if you prefer. They are braised slowly and you end up with a wonderful sauce redolent of orange and star anise. Serve with home-made pasta, such as fettuccine, for a complete meal.

6 plump duck maryland, trimmed of excess fat
olive oil
a knob of butter
salt and pepper
80 ml red wine
10 sage leaves
peel of ½ orange, all pith removed
3 pieces star anise
600 g Italian tomatoes, peeled and chopped

duck pieces in tomato, orange and star anise | serves 4–6

Trim the duck pieces and divide the thighs from the legs if you wish.
Heat some oil and butter in a large casserole pan and brown the duck pieces all over. Season with salt and pepper, then add the wine and simmer until evaporated.
Add the sage leaves, orange peel, star anise and tomatoes and braise slowly (set the lid so it sits askew) until the duck is tender and you have a wonderful fragrant sauce. You may need to add a little hot water if it seems to be drying out.

chicken alla veneta
serves 4–6

Call me crazy about chicken and, yes, I will agree. Here is a dish of braised chicken with potatoes. The potatoes provide texture and are ideal for soaking up the juices.

1 x 1.6 kg free-range or corn-fed chicken, cut into pieces at the joints
olive oil, for frying
1 onion, peeled and chopped
1 carrot, peeled and chopped
2 cloves garlic, chopped
3 slices pancetta or bacon
1 x 400 g tin tomatoes
4 medium-sized potatoes, peeled and cut into 2 cm cubes
20 small black olives
a small sprig of rosemary
salt and pepper

Prepare the chicken pieces and pat dry.
Heat the oil in a non-stick casserole pan. Add the vegetables and garlic and sauté until they soften and colour. Add the chicken and pancetta and brown lightly all over. Add the tomatoes, potatoes, olives and rosemary. Season with salt and pepper. Cover the pan, leaving the lid slightly askew. Simmer gently for around an hour, until the chicken is tender.

veal loin on the barbecue | serves 4
as part of a barbecue selection

Good veal is not easy to find, but if you have a friendly and keen butcher you may be in luck. The veal loin I suggest for this recipe is from an older animal rather than baby veal. It is a delicious meat, not ordinarily used for a barbecue. The secret to this dish is to not overcook it. So if you like your meat well done, then this may not be for you.

1 x 600 g veal loin
olive oil
a few sprigs of rosemary
best-quality extra-virgin olive oil
a squeeze of lemon juice
salt flakes
freshly cracked black pepper

Marinate the veal in olive oil and rosemary leaves for a few hours. Preheat the grill on your barbecue and grill the veal for a few minutes on all sides, so that it is cooked to about 1 cm inwards, leaving the centre pink. Remove from the heat and rest for at least 20 minutes in a warm place. Slice the veal and serve with a drizzle of olive oil, a squeeze of lemon juice, a sprinkle of salt flakes and some freshly cracked black pepper.

lamb cutlets with a hint of garlic
serves 4

In recent years lamb cutlets have become something of a luxury item, because the drought has driven up the price of lamb. In a sense this is a good thing, as it may mean that people will stop taking for granted Australia's greatest asset – lamb. These lamb cutlets are lovely served with a Green Bean and Cherry Tomato Salad (see page 141) and some warm focaccia.

16 lamb cutlets
olive oil
2 cloves garlic, peeled and roughly chopped
a few sprigs of rosemary
salt and pepper
best-quality extra-virgin olive oil

Marinate the cutlets for a couple of hours in the olive oil, garlic and rosemary. Grill quickly, preferably on the barbecue. Season with salt and pepper. Serve with your best extra-virgin olive oil on the table so everyone can help themselves.

Pigeon is readily available in most produce markets or can be ordered from your butcher. It is not a rare food for secret societies any more. It is also fairly easy to cook, so long as you remember to keep it rare if you are roasting it.

8 pigeons
white wine
sage leaves
olive oil
selection of salad leaves, including
    radicchio, cos or iceberg
a drizzle of extra-virgin olive oil
a splash of balsamic vinegar
salt and pepper

Cut the pigeons in half and marinate in a little white wine, sage leaves and olive oil for a few hours.

When you are ready to cook, preheat your grill or barbecue and preheat the oven to 200°C. Place a roasting tray in the oven to heat.

Grill the pigeons lightly so they colour all over. Transfer to the hot roasting tray and drizzle over a little oil. Roast for 8 minutes, or until pink.

Remove from the oven and rest the pigeons in a warm place. Use a sharp knife to slice away the breasts from the ribcage. Slice the breasts and arrange on each plate with a small mound of salad on the side, dressed with the olive oil and balsamic vinegar, and seasoned with salt and pepper. Add the legs as well, which are lovely to chew on.

sopa coada | pigeon soup
serves 6–8

A grand occasion dish, and a classic regional dish from my city, Treviso, near Venice. It is not elaborate, but it will take time and it requires the confidence of the more experienced cook. Sopa coada translates into something like 'slow-cooked', a bit like the way that birds incubate their eggs. Originally it was cooked very, very slowly in an earthenware dish in the oven. My version is a little more user-friendly.

6–8 pigeons
40 ml olive oil
2 carrots, peeled and chopped
2 onions, peeled and chopped
4 sticks celery, chopped
3 cloves garlic, chopped
a few leaves of sage and rosemary
1 bay leaf
250 ml red wine
2 litres Golden Chicken Stock (see page 79)
10 slices day-old bread from a rustic-style loaf
200 g parmesan, grated
good quality extra-virgin olive oil

Wash the pigeons and pat dry. Heat half the olive oil in a large, heavy-based casserole pan and sauté half the vegetables with the garlic and herbs until they soften and colour lightly. Add the pigeons and brown them all over. Add the red wine and simmer on a medium heat until it is reduced almost to nothing. Gradually add 1 litre of the chicken stock, so as not to reduce the temperature too much. Cover the pan, leaving the lid slightly askew, and simmer gently for around an hour, until the pigeon is tender and the meat can be easily removed from the bones and shredded. Keep the meat to one side and reserve the bones for the stock. Return the pan to the heat and simmer until the sauce reduces further. Pour through a fine sieve and refrigerate. Skim off any fat on the surface. Mix the sauce with the reserved pigeon meat. This may all be done ahead of time.

To make the stock, heat the remaining olive oil in a large heavy-based saucepan and sauté the remaining vegetables and the reserved pigeon bones until they are lightly browned. Add the remaining stock and simmer for at least an hour.

Preheat the oven to 120°C. Line a baking dish with some of the bread and top with some of the pigeon meat in its sauce. It should be a snug fit. Sprinkle generously with cheese and pour on enough of the stock to make the bread quite soggy. Add another layer of bread, meat and cheese and soak with more of the stock. Finish with a sprinkling of cheese. Cover with aluminium foil and bake for an hour. Remove the foil and return the dish to the oven to brown the top. Be very careful not to let it dry out; add a little more stock if necessary.

Serve in hot bowls with a good drizzle of your best olive oil.

lamb neck with peas
serves 4–6

This is an old favourite of mine. It takes some time to cook, but not your time, it's the oven's time.

3 lamb necks, split in half lengthwise and sinew removed
plain flour
olive oil
2 sticks celery, finely chopped
2 carrots, peeled and finely chopped
1 onion, peeled and finely chopped
3 cloves garlic, chopped
125 ml red wine
2 cups peeled, crushed tomatoes
1 litre lamb or beef stock (fairly concentrated)

Preheat the oven to 180°C.

Wash the necks well and remove any fat. Dry well and toss in a little flour. Shake off any excess, leaving only the lightest of coatings.

Heat some olive oil in a pan and seal the necks all over. Set aside.

In a baking dish, fry the vegetables and garlic in some oil. Add the necks, bone side down, and add the red wine. Let it evaporate. Add the tomatoes and stock. Cover the top with greased paper and foil.

Bake in the oven for a good 90 minutes. At that point, the meat should come off the bone. If not, cook it for longer, perhaps adding more stock. Remove the meat from the bone and set aside. Push the cooking liquid through a sieve and chill; the fat will come to the top. Discard the fat, heat the sauce and place the neck meat in it to warm up. Serves with mashed potatoes.

eat it raw I used to think beef was suss because I associated it with machismo and beer drinking – I have always felt uneasy about both. I guess I have also disliked it as the one-dimensional dietary preference of the majority, especially in its meat and three veg form. I mean, why be obsessed about steak when there is so much other food to enjoy? And why be obsessed about steak, anyway, when meat eaters could enjoy so many other parts of a cow?

During my early days in Australia, I could not escape the impression that steak and beer were not only a part of the national diet, but were also somehow connected to the notion of being a 'real man' and a real Aussie. Such an exaggerated perception certainly slowed down my real understanding of things, but then there are things that stick to the mind, like it or not, and colour your initial perceptions of your new neighbourhood. Beef or meat generally, I understood later, is an important part of the diet simply because this country has always produced an awful lot of it. And the fact that most people like it well done, by the way, is just the same as in every other country.

What concerns me about beef now are two other issues: the first is that given its abundance, people have forgotten how to use the non-prime cuts. The second – and perhaps the more important issue – is the difficulty in purchasing beef with a degree of confidence about its quality. We have all tended to rely on the trusted butcher – as one should – or on the price as a reflection of quality, but without any reliable guarantees. I have purchased, time and again, some premium cuts at a premium price only to be bitterly disappointed. The high cost of a product is not in itself a guarantee. This problem has preoccupied meat producers for quite some time and extensive programs are now being tested in the market place to come up with schemes that ensure that price and quality are roughly in proportion.

I once had a most interesting experience when, on a short Tasmanian trip, by chance I met the Hammond brothers, who run a cattle property on Robbins and Walker Islands and on the mainland, in the vicinity of Stanley. The Hammonds produce top of the range beef and would have no problems giving a cast iron guarantee about the quality of their meat. People like them are at the top of the quality pyramid. The only problem is that they tend to export almost everything they produce.

The Hammonds are lucky because their grandfather, James Holyman, had the foresight to purchase these two beautiful islands from the Van Diemen Land Company in 1916. (The islands were an original grant of King George IV to the Van Diemen Land Company.) The Holyman family were pioneers in shipping and aviation in Australia, having over 60 vessels in the early 1900s and starting and managing ANA airways before the company was bought by Sir Reginald Ansett in the late 1950s.

The islands are accessible at low tide by four-wheel drive vehicles or, I'd imagine, on foot. The trip from the mainland farm, along the beaches, with cattle, across Robbins Passage to Robbins Island, is 28 kilometres from paddock to paddock.

In these stunning landscapes, which are so typically Australian, the Hammonds run only Wagyu beef, commonly referred to as 'Kobe beef'. They prefer this Japanese breed of cattle for their ability to produce the most marbled meat in the world. Nearly all of their production, like many other good Tassie products, goes straight overseas where it fetches high prices.

I understand that a high price can put people off, but then many people are prepared to pay for lots of outrageously expensive habits, so why not pay more for beef that is outrageously good? The important thing, for me at least, would be to know that I can buy standard good quality beef, properly priced, or Wagyu or Angus or similar and pay accordingly.

I found myself grappling with one large piece of strip loin donated by the Hammonds for the 10 Days on the Island Festival event in Stanley and in the Stanley Golf Club kitchen, with a tiny electric domestic stove and the task of cooking for 140 people. When I sampled it myself, raw, not knowing what it was and who had given it, I was struck by a thunderbolt. I had never tasted anything like it in terms of flavour and texture. So I resolved, there and then, that the guests would eat it raw, which is what they did.

If you want to be a real man, then, eat it raw, I say! Raw beef is sometimes called 'carpaccio', a word that is now used for any raw food cut thinly. This method of presenting meat comes from Venice. Vittore Carpaccio was a sixteenth-century Venetian painter. For a carpaccio of beef it is preferable to use eye fillet, because it involves the least amount of waste. I have given a recipe for it on page 198.

It seems as if there is pork belly on every restaurant menu these days. Maybe because it is a very cheap cut of meat, or hopefully because people have seen the light. Pork belly may look fatty, but it is delicious and some of the fat is released in the very slow cooking. Once again, you have to do next to nothing.

I read recently that Americans have just discovered that lard contains less cholesterol than butter and less 'fat' than olive oil, so Italian lard is the current craze in the Big Apple. Next they will discover that pigeons lay eggs . . .

The ribs can be cooked into a tomato sauce. Extended slow cooking will break down the meat and the sauce will have great flavour.

2 kg pork belly, ribs removed
1 cup water
char siu sauce or hoisin sauce
2–3 cloves garlic, peeled and coarsely chopped
1 knob fresh ginger, peeled and coarsely chopped

slow-roasted pork belly | serves 6

Preheat the oven to 110°C.

Wash the pork belly and pat dry. Place in a heavy baking dish, skin down, and add the water. Spread a thin film of sauce evenly over the pork and sprinkle with the garlic–ginger mixture. Cover loosely with aluminium foil. Over the next 4 hours, the pork will rise like a soufflé, releasing some of its fat. Eventually it will collapse into a gelatinous, soft texture, redolent of Chinese flavours.

Serve the pork belly with a salad of thinly sliced cabbage dressed with a little balsamic vinegar and a drizzle of the pork cooking juices. Cucumber is also nice and refreshing, and steamed rice makes a good starch accompaniment to mop up the juices.

Veal liver with soft onions is an old Venetian recipe. The liver must be fresh and from a young animal, otherwise it can be a little strong-smelling. A trusted butcher should help you. Ask him to remove any sinewy bits and give you slices of about 5 cm by 1 cm. Use a non-stick pan if possible; the veal will cook very quickly – and it is best when left a little pink.

olive oil

butter

3 medium-sized brown onions, thinly sliced

20 slices veal liver

salt and pepper

a few drops of balsamic vinegar

veal liver with onions | serves 4

Heat some olive oil and butter in a frying pan and gently sauté the onions for 20 minutes or so, until they soften and collapse to a lovely golden-brown heap. Add a little water or stock from time to time to keep them moist. Remove from the pan and set aside.

Heat a little more oil and butter in the pan and quickly sauté the liver until brown on all sides. Season with salt and pepper. The cooking should only take a few minutes. Add a splash of balsamic vinegar and return the onions to the pan to warm through. Eat immediately with a little wilted spinach or grilled polenta.

carpaccio di filetto
serves 4

Strictly speaking, carpaccio is served raw. Most restaurants freeze the meat and use an industrial slicer to achieve the desired wafer-thin pink slices. I suggest you sear it briefly all over, which will make it easier to slice thinly.

extra-virgin olive oil
1 x 400 g beef eye fillet, cut from
   the centre
salt flakes
freshly ground black pepper

Heat a frying pan to get it really hot. Add a little oil and the beef fillet and sear the meat briefly on all sides. You only need to lightly brown the outside. Remove from the pan and leave to cool. Slice as finely as possible. Serve with a drizzle of extra-virgin olive oil, a sprinkling of salt and a grind of cracked black pepper. It is also delicious with a light caper mayonnaise and a few red and white leaves of witlof.

ossobuco
serves 4

Ossobuco – or the bone with the hole – is traditionally served with saffron risotto.

8 or more pieces of ossobuco
plain flour, for dusting
olive oil
butter
1 large onion, peeled and chopped
2 medium-sized carrots, peeled and
   chopped
2 sticks celery, chopped
salt and pepper
150 ml red wine
1 x 400 g tin tomatoes, or 400 g ripe
   fresh tomatoes, chopped
1 litre Golden Chicken Stock (see
   page 79) or hot water
grated zest of 1 lemon
1 clove garlic, peeled and
   finely chopped
2 tablespoons finely chopped
   flat-leaf parsley

Dust the ossobuco in flour. Heat some olive oil and butter in a frying pan and seal the ossobuco, a few at a time, until they are lightly browned all over. Heat a little more oil in a large heavy-based casserole and lightly fry the vegetables until lightly browned. Add the ossobuco and season with salt and pepper. Add the wine and simmer until the juices evaporate. Add the tomatoes and simmer very gently with the lid on for a couple of hours on top of the stove. Add a little water or stock if the meat looks as if it might be drying out.
When ready to serve, combine the lemon zest, garlic and parsley, and sprinkle over the ossobuco.

braised oxtail
serves 4–5

I love this recipe because it goes well either with pasta or mashed potato. A savvy cook will know that oxtail is economical, easy to cook and full of flavour.

1 kg oxtail, cut into pieces
olive oil
1 onion, peeled and chopped
1 carrot, peeled and chopped
1 stick celery, chopped
2 cloves garlic, peeled and chopped
1 glass red wine
a small piece of orange peel
1 x 400 g tin tomatoes
salt and pepper
500 g pasta
freshly grated Parmigiano or Romano
chopped flat-leaf parsley

Blanch the oxtail in boiling water. Heat the olive oil in a large casserole and sauté the vegetables and garlic until they soften and brown. Add the blanched oxtail, followed by the wine. Simmer for a few minutes to evaporate. Add the orange peel and tomatoes and season with salt and pepper. Cover the pan and simmer on a very low heat for 2–3 hours, or until the meat is falling off the bone. If the meat looks like it is drying out, add a little hot stock or water.
When ready to serve, cook the pasta in plenty of boiling salted water until al dente. Drain and serve with the oxtail, a handful of grated cheese, a little chopped parsley and with a big salad on the side.

formaggio

italian cheese

cheese is fundamental to Italian cooking and eating. I cannot comprehend how people can cook pasta and omit the cheese, seriously overlooking the intimate relationship between pasta, sauce and cheese. There is also a growing lack of knowledge and about cheese in general, a fact related, in my opinion, to the industrialisation of cheese. Consumers have succumbed to the lure of processed cheese, in the same manner as they have with bread. They are happy with what I call 'plastic' cheese, that ubiquitous slice of indigestible material that's pushed into children's lunches, some sandwiches and melted into toasts or burgers.

There is nothing less than an international conspiracy led by multinationals to eliminate any trace of real cheese made from raw milk. In order to conquer the world with artificial cheese, the health factor has been agitated by smart manipulators of people's basic fears: eat raw milk cheese and, if you are pregnant, your baby will die! This is terrorism, aided and abetted, among others, by the Australian and New Zealand regulators. As a result we cannot import certain traditional European cheese and, more importantly, we cannot make domestic cheese with raw milk. Milk must be pasteurised if you want to make legal Australian cheese and in doing so certain basic elements of flavour – ultimately it is all about flavour – and texture cannot be achieved. The regulators and manufacturers would be happy if there were only a few types of cheese, made like plastic, easily transportable with long life – read shelf life – achieved by eliminating any sign of life in the cheese.

For this state of affairs I am pointing the finger at ignorant politicians, who have not taken an interest in this issue. Any politician who pretends to be interested in food is no more than just another accomplice in the destruction of cheese.

I am pointing the finger to the Ministers for Health and Agriculture who are happy to sell out Australia's overall best interests to conform to the wishes of US Food and Agriculture lobby.

I am pointing the finger at faceless bureaucrats and regulators who go to work without any passion or interest in the very matter they are supposed to regulate. They are the very same people who want to flog us genetically modified foods, even BEFORE knowing what the consequences will be. These are the people who enforced the destruction of a consignment of Roquefort cheese because it is made with raw milk. The French, avid consumers of cheese, must be impressed by the fact that their food is illegal in our country! The very same regulator tried to enforce a ban on the import of Parmigiano, which simply would have led to a revolt by the Italian community in Australia. Has anybody ever seen anyone getting sick from eating Parmigiano? I would have a nervous breakdown without it! And where is the famous freedom of choice? Why are cigarettes and alcohol being sold, but not cheese from raw milk? I sometimes get the feeling that I'm living in an insane Kafka-like world of nightmares.

Pietro Sardo of Slow Food says that in Europe real cheese is also under threat, much for the same reasons: 'globalisation demands large quantities, competitive price, a continuous production cycle and guaranteed hygiene, so, in practice, EC legislation has enshrined the interests of food multinationals in community law. Consumers have been willing accomplices. They have betrayed local products for the siren song of hypermarkets' refrigerated counters. The cheeses people buy in these outlets are sanitised, odourless and made from machines that spit them out as if they were a die-cast'. The issue of cheese points, once again, to the need for a Ministry for Food, one central agency to deal with all policy matters relating to food. Ultimately there should be only one port of call, rather than a myriad of organisations working with subterfuge and able to conveniently disappear from public view. If there were a Minister for Food, powerful lobbies may even be more successful at corrupting processes, but at least corruption would become transparent. At the moment, insidious regulations are passed without thinking people being even remotely aware of them or their consequences.

There are some popular names when it comes to Italian cheese: mozzarella, ricotta, mascarpone, provolone, pecorino, grana, Parmigiano Reggiano, gorgonzola (dolce and piccante), taleggio, asiago and fontina. These types of cheese have become part of our culinary language here in Australia, even though in reality often these cheeses only share the name with the real thing.

The purpose of this chapter is to provide a quick overview of how some cheeses are used in cooking and on a cheese platter, and why their imitation should be avoided altogether.

Parmigiano Reggiano The 'king' of cheese as far as I am concerned, and one with the most application in the kitchen, besides being good eating as is. Grated, shaved or in lumps, this is, for me, the indispensable ingredient, a defining flavour of Italian cuisine. First of all, the name 'parmesan' on anything means nothing – it can be very poor quality cheese. Parmigiano Reggiano is a very precise cheese made under very precise rules set out by the producers back in 1934. It can only be made in five specific provinces, outside of which the cheese is not Parmigiano Reggiano. This is a hard cooked cheese that has matured for at least 14 months. Those going to three years are called stravecchio, or very old Parmigiano Reggiano; they display tiny sweet crystals and are best purchased from a big wheel.

Throughout this book I have used Parmigiano Reggiano in just about every recipe. Parmigiano is what soy sauce or ginger are to the Chinese. A risotto al Parmigiano Reggiano is simply a risotto with chicken stock flavoured at the end with a generous amount of Parmigiano Reggiano. This is delicate food for people who feel like a gentle dish, like spaghetti with butter and Parmigiano Reggiano.

40 g butter
40 ml olive oil
1 small brown onion, finely diced
200 g Italian risotto rice
2 litres Golden Chicken Stock (see page 79), kept simmering
salt and pepper
butter
Parmigiano Reggiano
a squeeze of lemon juice (optional)

risotto in bianco al parmigiano | serves 4

Heat the butter and oil in a heavy-based pan and cook the onion until soft. Add the rice and toast it by frying it until it has absorbed all the fat.

After a minute or so, begin adding the hot stock, a ladleful at a time, stirring constantly. As the risotto is cooking, be careful to not drown the rice or allow it to become too dry. Cook for 15–20 minutes, or until the rice is cooked, but each grain is still slightly firm in the centre. Season lightly. Remove from the heat and stir in some butter and a generous amount of cheese. The idea is for a good, clean parmesan flavour. Cover for 2 minutes to allow the butter and cheese to be absorbed, then serve. Add a squeeze of lemon juice just before serving if you want to.

parmigiano with treviso mustard

This is more a suggestion than a recipe. Veneto mustard fruits are different from any other simply because this conserve is rather thick and less sweet. It suits the flavour of Parmigiano, so I suggest that you eat a small piece of Parmigiano with a small amount of mustard. The combination is a real winner!

grana

Grana can be used in the same way as Parmigiano, but as it is less expensive it can be used in everyday dishes and not just kept for special occasions. The milk for grana – which means grainy – is collected from 27 provinces in the northern Italian plains known as Pianura Padana. Grana is a more commercial cheese and therefore the quality may very enormously. In Australia it is often sold far too fresh and it is usually price-driven. If it is semi-soft it is best to ignore it, unless you really have no choice.

brodo, bread and grana
serves 6

A recipe similar to Pasta in Brodo (see page 79), except that instead of pasta you use good quality bread – preferably a couple of days old. The grana lumps melt in the hot stock while the bread 'bulks' up the soup. Naturally, this is just as good, if not better, without the bread.

1.5 litres Golden Chicken Stock
   (see page 79)
4 small slices good quality rustic-style
   bread, left to go stale
Grana Padano cheese, grated and
   also in small lumps

Heat the stock, add the bread and the cheese and serve really hot.

ricotta is the first of the specialist cheeses made by migrant communities in the urban centres of Australia. Long before it became fashionable to cook with or simply eat specialist cheeses from the many regions of Australia, there were 'true believers' working in the industrial suburbs of the major cities making their own versions of ricotta, mozzarella and other cheeses permitted by the regulations.

Some would say that ricotta is not really a cheese, because it is made from whey, which is actually a by-product of cheese-making. To make the cheese, milk is curdled with rennet. Not all of the milk turns to cheese, and some protein escapes into the residual liquid called the whey. When whey is re-cooked (hence the word ricotta – 'cotta' means cooked in Italian) and some acid is added, a delicate curd is formed. This is ricotta, characteristically low in fat, soft or well drained, depending on the type and naturally quite 'sweet'.

Not all ricotta made in Australia is obtained completely from the whey. Manufacturers tend to add more milk or milk in powder form to make a richer, fattier curd. If you read the ingredients list you'll be able to find out which ricotta is made with what milk. The addition of extra milk of either kind tends to increase the fat content, so if you're looking for low-fat ricotta you must be careful with your choice. Non-artisan ricotta is made with semi-skimmed milk, and this product can sometimes be gritty and unpleasant. I have often found it impossible to cook with gritty, lumpy or wet ricotta or one that has a combination of all three faults. With such immense variation, when you see a recipe calling for ricotta, be careful about what you buy. 'Use the best ingredients possible' is one of those phrases that is particularly relevant when it concerns the use of ricotta in the kitchen. Ricotta is an essential ingredient in Italian cooking.

Its texture, especially when made properly, is delicate and light. This non-cheese takes on the flavour of other ingredients, both savoury and sweet. Hence ricotta is delicious when mixed with blanched spinach to go into a classic ravioli or cannelloni. It is equally delicious if you don't care about fat – when whisked into double cream and served with honey, or candied orange peel, almond, sugar or rose water. Ricotta mixes well with chocolate, and sultanas, too. It can be supported or surrounded by shortcrust pastry, as in the many variations of *torta di ricotta*, including the famous pastiera napoletana – a ricotta tart containing wheat boiled in sugar and milk (see page 73).

One of my favourites is homemade fettuccine, dressed with a traditional Bolognese sauce, grated parmesan, fresh ricotta and a pinch of cinnamon.

An Indian friend of mine makes a rich tomato sauce with ginger and garlic, fries thick ricotta slices in oil until brown, and places the cheese back into the sauce, finishing off the dish with coriander sprigs.

making ricotta

ricotta gnocchi
serves 6

If you want to try making a curd cheese similar to ricotta, try the following method. Add 3 drops of lemon juice to 3 litres full-fat milk and leave in a cool place (not the refrigerator) for 36 hours. Place the acidulated milk in a large pan with 250 ml plain yoghurt and bring to boiling point for 1 minute. As the milk boils, scoop out the curds and drain in a colander or sieve. This simple curd makes nice dumplings when mixed with eggs, breadcrumbs and grated cheese and cooked in a tomato sauce.

Ask for your ricotta to be cut from a large round – it's usually firmer.

2 cups ricotta, drained
1½ cups grated parmesan, plus
    extra to serve
1½ cups plain flour
5 tablespoons broken up gorgonzola,
    or a similar blue cheese
4 tablespoons butter
a few splashes of cream
freshly ground black pepper

Mix the ricotta and parmesan, and add enough flour to make a firm but soft dough. Using a tablespoon, shape the dough into dumplings about the size of a walnut. Cook in salted boiling water for 6–8 minutes, by which time the gnocchi should float to the top. Scoop them out with a slotted spoon or tip into a colander. In a small non-stick pan melt the blue cheese and butter with the cream. Add the gnocchi and cook for a few moments, stirring gently to combine. Add more parmesan and pepper, and serve immediately.

mascarpone

Like ricotta, mascarpone is a critical ingredient in Italian cooking, most notably for the famous tiramisu, but also as an alternative to cream in sweet and savoury dishes. Mascarpone is not exactly a cheese, as it is not set using a traditional curdling agent. But it is not a butter.

To make mascarpone, cream is heated to 100°C and citric acid is introduced to curdle it. It is then left to hang in a muslin bag for several days.

crema al mascarpone con crostoli
serves 6

A mascarpone cream is luscious and decadent. It is in fact the same mixture as goes into a tiramisu.

4 eggs, separated
1 tablespoon caster sugar or
    more to taste
250 g mascarpone

Beat the egg yolks with sugar until fluffy. Add the mascarpone and beat on a low speed until well incorporated. Transfer to a large mixing bowl.
Beat the egg whites till they form soft peaks. Do not overbeat. Gently but swiftly incorporate the whites into the mascarpone mixture. Add enough for the cream to be light, but not runny. Much will depend on the quality and density of the mascarpone.
I like serving this cream with marinated strawberries. Place strawberries in a bowl and mix with a little sugar and a liqueur of your choice. In the summer this is a truly delightful dessert. Otherwise dunk the crostoli into this cream.

tiramisu
serves 6 or more

An old classic. Many towns in Italy have claimed it as their own, but I am assured that it originated in Treviso. The owner of the oldest restaurant there, Le Beccherie, simply said to me, 'I wish I had registered the name "tiramisu" when my parents were serving this dessert in the 1960s – I would be rich now.' Use a good quality cocoa powder – definitely not drinking chocolate.

4 eggs, separated
2 tablespoons caster sugar or
    more to taste
250 g mascarpone
12 savoiardi biscuits (chunky ones,
    not thin and light)
250 ml strong black coffee
40 ml Marsala
cocoa powder for dusting

Beat the egg yolks with 1 tablespoon sugar until fluffy. Add the mascarpone and beat on a low speed until well incorporated. Transfer to a bowl.
Beat the egg whites and the other tablespoon of sugar till they form peaks. Gently incorporate the whites into the mascarpone mixture.
Dip the savoiardi in the coffee one at a time, making sure they absorb the coffee but are not saturated.
Arrange half the biscuits in the bottom of a small container and cover with bit of marsala. Form a second layer with the remaining biscuits and mascarpone and marsala. Allow to sit for 2 hours in the fridge before eating. Dust with cocoa before serving.

A semifreddo is almost like an ice-cream, but it does not need churning. A silky semifreddo is obtained by cooking the eggs whites (beaten to firm peaks) with a caramel at 120°C. Technically, you should have a sugar thermometer, which isn't expensive to buy, but you can risk this recipe by doing without.

Set the semifreddo in a log-shaped mould – from which you cut pretty slices – or small plastic dariole moulds or indeed coffee cups – there is no law that says you have to unmould the dessert. Your home is not a restaurant!

6 egg whites
200 g caster sugar
100 ml water
250 g cream
250 g mascarpone
20 unsalted, shelled pistachios

semifreddo al mascarpone | serves 10

First, make an Italian meringue. Beat the egg whites with 100 g of the sugar to firm peaks. Meanwhile, boil the remaining 100 g sugar with the water until it is bubbling and the water has evaporated. This is hard to judge, but you should be able to see that there has been a reduction in the level of the liquid. At this point the sugar should still be white and syrupy. If it has started to change colour, you have gone too far. If you use a sugar thermometer, you can't go wrong – just work to 120°C. Pour the sugar syrup in a steady stream onto the beaten egg whites, beating on a medium speed so that the mixture cools as it is beaten. Place the bowl in the fridge to cool completely.

Beat the cream to soft peaks and gently mix in the mascarpone. When the meringue is cold, fold it into the mascarpone cream. Fold in the pistachios, which add a nice bit of colour. Pour the semifreddo into moulds of your choice and freeze.

This is a fairly rich dessert and only needs some fresh fruit to accompany it. In the photograph it is served with pistachio praline. Make the praline by stirring pistachios into caramel and pouring into a lightly oiled metal tray. When the caramel sets, crush finely and use as a sweet garnish for desserts.

mozzarella

There are many types of mozzarella, which is essentially a fresh cheese that can be soft or semi-hard. The word mozzarella derives from the word *mozzare*, which means to tear or pull. This refers to the process of making this type of fresh cheese, and precisely to the point where the expert cheese-maker begins to pull and stretch the elastic mass of curd so that the outer layer forms the skin within which the soft curd is found. Each ball is then placed in a cold brine solution. What you get then is a ball containing moist, milky layers of spun curd covered with a thin rind.

In Australia, unfortunately, mozzarella is usually a tasteless, grated concoction made for the cheap pizza market. It is possibly one of our major exports for the growing international craving for pizza, especially in Japan. Over the last twenty years, this vulgar cheese has been somewhat substituted in the kitchen with 'bocconcini', which are, I guess, an improvement.

Bocconcini – or fior di latte (flower of the milk) – is fresh stretched curd cheese sold uncured, resting in a salty brine. Buffalo mozzarella is made with buffalo milk. It has a distinctive soft, spongy texture, which absorbs oil easily, as in the dish insalata caprese. Mozzarella also goes into dishes such as parmigiana di melanzane, because it melts well. Buffalo mozzarella is made in Australia and I believe it is also possible to purchase imported ones. It may be a little dear, but worth the experience. Technically, this is the only real fresh mozzarella. It dates back to time immemorial, to the swampy, malarial areas near Naples and it was not as highly regarded as it is now.

insalata caprese
serves 4

2 buffalo mozzarella
4 ripe tomatoes
salt and pepper
extra-virgin olive oil
12 basil leaves

Slice the mozzarella and the
tomatoes. Arrange on a plate in
overlapping layers. Season well with
salt and pepper, and drizzle
generously with oil. Scatter on the
basil leaves and serve.

eggplant parmigiana
serves 10 or more

Another classic dish that can be
eaten hot or cold in the summer
months when eggplant are in season.
When you embark on this dish, there
is no point making a small one, so I
suggest a 30 cm x 40 cm baking dish
or thereabouts.

8 medium-sized eggplant
plain flour, for dusting
oil, for frying
500 g fresh mozzarella
800 ml Tomato Sauce (see page 153)
salt and pepper
basil leaves
200 g Grana Padano, grated
breadcrumbs (optional)

Cut the eggplant lengthwise into
4 mm slices and dust very lightly
with flour. Heat a generous amount of
oil in a large, heavy-based frying pan
and sauté the eggplant on both sides
to a nice golden colour. Remove from
the pan and drain on kitchen paper.
Slice the mozzarella and reserve.
Preheat the oven to 180°C.
Spread a little tomato sauce on the
bottom of a baking dish. Arrange a
layer of eggplant slices on the sauce,
season with salt and pepper and top
with slices of mozzarella. Scatter on
a few basil leaves and some grated
cheese. Repeat the layering until
ll the ingredients have been used.
Top with extra cheese and the
breadcrumbs if using, and bake for
35 minutes until piping hot.

provolone

This cheese can be mild or 'piccante'
(sharp) and is typical of Southern
Italy, although these days masses of
it are produced in the north of Italy.
Besides being good to eat, when of
good reputable quality, it can liven up
some soups, frittata, tarts and various
stuffings.
Provolone, Provole, Caciocavallo and
Scamorza are all mature stretched-
curd cheeses. Hot whey and water are
used to scald the curds in order to
firm them and prevent further acid
development. The water added is at
90–95°C. This makes the curds melt
and consolidate into a thick, fibrous,
pliable mass. The warm curd mass is
kneaded until it is smooth and shiny,
then cut into long pieces and pulled
into long threads.
By comparison with mozzarella, these
harder stretched cheese types are
worked more intensively to expel
moisture. They come in many shapes,
from giant sausages, to cones, to
bells and pear shapes. As they age
they can become more 'piccante'.

The most concentrated and driest forms of cheese are the hard cooked ones such as Parmigiano Reggiano and pecorino. The curd for these cheeses is cut finely, and then it is cooked and scalded at a high temperature. The result is a dry and dense mass, but not a brittle one. The external surface is oiled to form a rind and maturation occurs over a year in a warm place.

Pecorino is an ewe's milk cheese. It is also regional, coming from places such as Lazio (Pecorino Romano), Tuscany (Toscano) or Sardinia (Sardo). What's upsetting about most Australian pecorino is that, with a few notable exceptions, it is made with cow's milk. Once again, this abominable practice goes to show that buying and using cheese requires one to be alert and street-wise.

Essentially this is the same recipe for Broad Bean Stew on page 138 except that here the tomatoes are excluded and the broad beans are covered with a light stock or simply with water. At the end, small cubes of provolone are added and the soup is served with crostini.

In the summer when basil is aplenty, it is time to make beautiful pesto, which goes well with home-made pasta, especially stracci. These are literally pasta 'rags' which are obtained by roughly cutting a smooth pasta sheet. The unevenness of the pasta is particularly suited to a pesto sauce. The beauty of this dish comes from the smart use of a good pecorino cheese, which is more salty than most other hard cheeses.

pesto

80 g pine nuts

1 clove garlic, peeled

2 bunches basil, leaves only

200 ml extra-virgin olive oil, not too bitter

100 g pecorino toscano cheese, grated

stracci

80 g wafer-thin slices potato, about 2 mm thickness, virtually see-through

300 g Egg Pasta (see page 77), cut into roughly shaped pieces

80 g green beans, strings removed and pre-cooked until *al dente*

freshly grated pecorino

extra-virgin olive oil

stracci ai pesto | serves 4

To make the Pesto, put the pine nuts and garlic in the food processor and pulse. Add the basil and pulse, adding the oil gradually, until all ingredients are combined to a nice, creamy consistency. Add the cheese at the end and a little more oil if required.

Bring a large pan of salted water to the boil. Add the potatoes and pasta and cook for a couple of minutes, until the pasta is soft and silky. As long as the potato slices are thin enough, they should be cooked in this time too.

Place half of the pesto in a serving bowl with a couple of tablespoons of the pasta cooking water. Toss in the pasta, potatoes and beans and stir to combine. Add more pesto until it is the consistency you like and finish with extra cheese and a drizzle of oil, to taste.

Gorgonzola – a cheese I rank as important as Parmigiano Reggiano, even though it has fewer applications besides eating. The flavour of freshly made egg fettuccine with a gorgonzola sauce is one of life's great, simple pleasures. Also, polenta and gorgonzola I would choose as the food to take to the moon if I were to live there for a long time!

Gorgonzola refers to the town from where this cheese originates. It is a blue cheese. The spores of a blue mould *penicillium gorgonzola* are introduced into two curds, one from the evening's milk and one from the following morning's. The mixing of two curds causes the large gaps that are visible in gorgonzola and it is in these gaps that the blue mould develops. Gorgonzola is aged in cool and humid underground facilities.

There is traditional gorgonzola, called piccante, and there is a second version, made only from one vat of milk, which is sweeter. It lacks the complexity of the piccante, but obviously it appeals to many. In Australia, buyers should beware of any gorgonzola not sold from a large wheel as it may be too old. One common problem is when you notice a significant darkening near the. outer surface – that is a sign the cheese is old and oxidised and it's likely it'll be too salty.

Fettuccine al gorgonzola is not a dish for the faint-hearted, as it contains a large number of calories. However, you only need a little of it, and if followed by a salad it is not so bad . . .

50 g butter
50 ml cream or milk
100 g gorgonzola dolce
300 g Egg Pasta (see page 77), cut into fettuccine
4 tablespoons grated Parmigiano Reggiano

fettuccine al gorgonzola | serves 4

Melt the butter, cream and gorgonzola in a saucepan on a low heat.
Cook the fettuccine until *al dente* and toss in the sauce. Top with freshly grated Parmigiano to taste.

Panna cotta has been the desert of the 1990s. Infinite variations have been made and people never seem to tire of it. In this recipe it is flavoured with gorgonzola and honey and served with poached quinces.

Increase the gelatine to 6 g (3 sheets) if you fear it will not set. In that case, remove from the fridge before serving so that it comes to room temperature.

1 litre cream
30 g or more gorgonzola
80 g honey
a few coffee beans
10 cm orange peel
4 g gelatine (2 sheets)

panna cotta with gorgonzola and honey | serves 10

Put all the ingredients except the gelatine into a large saucepan and bring to just under the boil. Remove from the heat and leave to cool slightly.

Soften the gelatine in a little water, squeeze and add to the cream mixture. Strain through a fine sieve. Taste for sweetness and add a little more honey if you like.

When the mixture is cold, pour into lightly greased dariole moulds or small ramekin dishes and refrigerate. If you don't have suitable moulds you can simply spoon it straight from a large bowl. It may not look as elegant but it will do. The panna cotta should have a faint and pleasant taste of gorgonzola.

pastry

150 g unsalted butter, well chilled

250 g plain flour

1/2 teaspoon salt

1/2 cup cold water

1 egg white, beaten

filling

2 cups pumpkin, peeled and cut into small pieces

salt

sage leaves

4 eggs

400 ml cream

4 tablespoons gorgonzola

pumpkin tart with gorgonzola | serves 8 or more

To make the Pastry, cut the cold butter into small cubes. Rub with the flour and salt, or mix in a food processor to a breadcrumb texture. Add enough chilled water to form a pastry. Wrap in clingfilm and place in the refrigerator for an hour to rest.

Grease a 24 cm tart tin. Roll the dough out on a lightly floured work surface and line the prepared tart tin. Return to the fridge for another hour.

Preheat the oven to 160°C.

Line the tart shell with baking paper and dried beans or rice (or pastry weights) and blind-bake for 30–45 minutes. When the sides are cooked, remove from the oven and remove the beans or rice. Prick the base of the tart and brush with a little egg white, then return to the oven for another 30 minutes until the pastry shell has dried out.

To prepare the Filling, drizzle the pumpkin with a little olive oil, a sprinkling of salt and a few sage leaves. Roast in an oven preheated to 180°C until soft and lightly caramelised.

Place the pumpkin in the cooked shell. Mix the eggs and cream and gently pour over the pumpkin. Drop the gorgonzola here and there over the pumpkin and bake at 160°C until the egg and cream is set. Let cool and serve with a delicate salad.

taleggio

Taleggio is a soft cheese originating from Lombardy in the north of Italy. It is also a washed rind cheese, perhaps the only one in Italy. It has been matured over the centuries in the caves of the Val Sassina, where the microclimate suits its maturation process.

Taleggio as a name is a relatively recent invention. It was probably known as stracchino, from the word stracco, meaning tired, as the cows were after descending from the Alpine valleys before the onset of winter. There are not many good taleggios around in Australia, so once again you must look out for a reputable one like Mauri, which also makes the best gorgonzola. Look for a thin rind, lightly flecked with pinkish brown and dusted with white mould. It should be mature when it begins to show signs of oozing around the edge.

risotto di patate e taleggio
serves 4

40 g butter
40 ml olive oil
1 small brown onion, peeled and
   finely diced
3 medium-sized potatoes, peeled and
   finely diced
200 g Italian risotto rice
2 litres Golden Chicken Stock (see
   page 79), kept simmering
salt and pepper
120 g taleggio
Grana Padano
a few sage leaves

Heat the butter and oil in a heavy-based pan and cook the onion and potatoes for a few minutes. Add the rice and toast it by frying it until it has absorbed all the fat.

After a minute or so, begin to add the hot stock, a ladleful at a time, stirring constantly. As the risotto is cooking, be careful not to drown the rice or allow it to become too dry.

Cook for 15–20 minutes, or until the rice is cooked, but each grain is still slightly firm in the centre. Season lightly. Remove from the heat and stir in the taleggio, grana padano and sage leaves. Cover for 2 minutes to allow the cheese to be amalgamated, then serve.

fontina

Authentic fontina comes from the upper north-west of Italy in the region of Valle d'Aosta. It is a melting cheese that is often eaten in soft polenta or even on pizza. I understand it is now impossible – read illegal – to import fontina. You may find a replacement like a raclette, although it has a very different taste. To adapt this recipe, consult a cheese specialist about what would be a good substitute.

fonduta
serves 4

400 g cubed fontina
200 g milk
20 g butter
4 egg yolks

Place fontina in a bowl and cover with milk. Macerate for at least 2 hours. Melt the butter in a small stainless steel bowl set over warm water. Add the fontina and milk, and heat gently until the cheese has melted. Add the egg yolks, one by one, stirring to combine. Pour into bowls and serve with crostini and black pepper.

Fresh asiago is likely to come from pasteurised milk. Asiago is in the category of semi-hard cheeses, although that can mean different things. Ageing starts at three months or nine months and more. The older Asiago is actually good for grating. Together with Parmigiano Reggiano, taleggio, gorgonzola, fontina, montasio, provolone Grana Padano and Pecorino Romano, asiago is accredited under the DOC system. This was introduced after World War II to protect the integrity of certain products, like wine and cheese, so that the benchmark ones could not be spoiled by rogue imitations and substitutions.

The town of Asiago, set on a plateau above Vicenza, has provided many migrants to Australia, particularly to Melbourne. It is a typical mountain cheese. I love it with grilled white polenta and glass of light red.

Make a polenta according to page 112 and cool in a tray. Cut some slices and grill until brown and slightly charred. While still hot, place over it slices of asiago. Eat at once with a light red.

vino

italian wine

a long time ago, I had the misfortune of being asked by a friend in the wine industry to stand in on his behalf at a function of retired engineers to speak on the subject of Italian wines. The 'old boys' received me most kindly, but could not hide very well the fact that they did not believe a word I said. Any public speaker knows the dread of being looked at in a bemused fashion by a bunch of guys who want to laugh you out of court! They could not disagree with the content of Burton's voluminous book on Italian wines, from which I was quoting extensively. They could not argue with the fact that in antiquity, Italy was called Enotria, the country of wine, and that to this date it boasts over 2000 wine varieties, and that it is a major player in the world wine market. What these chaps could not accept and believe was the suggestion that Italian wines could be drunk. 'They are rubbish, they have no guts, they are not like our Rutherglen wines, they are not like Barossa shiraz,' and so on and on – was their refrain. The conversation retained a semblance of civility, but if ever I was trying to persuade them to my point of view, the mission was a failure. In hindsight, it is not surprising that the audience did not believe me. Italy had been a major producer of co-op wines made to a cheap formula and designed for bulk export.

More recently Italy has cleaned up its act. Wines exported these days are cleaner, fresher and defined by the specific character of their clone in conjunction with a clever matching to *terroir* and nearly always correct handling of oak. Way, way above all, they are marvellous when paired with the food of their region of origin. They are intriguing because they are nothing like what Australians have been used to – not by name, not by flavour.

The new generation of Australian drinkers does not have nasty memories of bad wines, not only from Italy, mind you, but from home as well. Hence they are better informed, more sophisticated, more open to suggestions.

A number of Australian growers now plant Italian varieties and a significant number of wineries vinify them. Pinot Grigio has recently become a household name. Sangiovese has wriggled its way into the extremely popular Rosemount split label range. Viognier is a loud instrument in the Yalumba orchestra. Nebbiolo seems to have found a home in the Victorian King Valley, together with Barbera and Arneis.

How did this trend begin? There is no possibility of a definitive history here, but there are discernible patches of development. For instance, many migrants brought pieces of vine-cane in their pockets, evidence of which exists in the King Valley. CSIRO keeps an extensive planting of vines from around the world, a kind of vine-library. Montrose was one of the first Australian wine companies to produce a Barbera and a Sangiovese, possibly out of 'material' found in Mudgee.

Coriole in the MacLaren Vale as well as Cherise were among the first producers of South Australian Sangiovese. Joe Grilli moved things along with a wine made in the Veneto style – a concentrated cabernet in he fashion of Amarone from the Verona area – while in Victoria Gary Crittenden was busy preparing the 'I' series, a range of Italian wines that really showed great affinity to food as well as hitherto unseen flavours. This trend is continuing, most definitely, and not just with Italian wines. Tempranillo, Monastrel and Graciano from Spain and Viognier and Petit Verdot from France have definitely joined the crowd of newcomers.

As the former Chairman of the Australian Alternative Varieties Wine Show Committee, I can say that I have witnessed first-hand the growth of these new varieties. The first show held only five years ago in Mildura saw a competition between some 27 wines, mostly pure Sangioveses or in a blend. The show now has over 300 entries from a rich diversity of varieties and regions, including New Zealand.

It is hard to guess what the future holds, but if experience teaches us anything, Australian growers and wineries will always be looking for something else, something that can give them a competitive advantage. There are many parts of Australia where we have yet to see plantings of new varieties; we do not know what the real potential for quality is – we have not yet experimented enough.

There are also many varieties that have not been planted at all as yet and if they have, it must be happening as I write. Vermentino, a lovely variety from Sardinia and Tuscany, comes to mind. I can also think of Negroamaro from Puglia and Nero d'Avola from Sicily. Many clones of Sangiovese, such as the famous 'Brunello,' which gives us the mighty Brunello di Montalcino, have yet to hit the ground. Chianti is made with Sangiovese. In some instances, the Sangiovese base is expanded with the help of small quantities of complementary grapes in the same clonal family such as colorino and canaiolo. Should Australian-grown Sangiovese also be blended with its brothers? Your guess is as good as mine.

As you'd expect, some of the newcomers are terrific and some are eminently forgettable. If the correct clone has been planted and care has been taken in the field and in the winery, then the results can be very good. Many gold medals were awarded to Pinot Grigio/Gris, to Viognier and to Petit Verdot. More than an encouraging result came for Nebbiolo grown and made in the King Valley (Pizzinis), and for an obscure Lagrein from Macedon (Cobaw Ridge), but overall Italian reds are not yet brilliant – at least in the context of the show. Some of these plantings may still yield a wine that is cheap and cheerful, and pleasant at a noisy party. The important thing is not to charge ridiculous amounts for these bulk producers.

The question of affordability opens another Pandora's box. Affordable wines can be made where the land is cheap, where there is access to water and certain economies of scale can be implemented. This actually is a roundabout way of saying that irrigated vineyards of the Murray region and the Riverina are capable of producing those wines that you reach for in your fridge almost daily, those that you can purchase around the $10–15 mark. Like it or not, the only place we can make drinkable wines at an affordable price is in the irrigated regions. Everyone knows that the cost of land these days determines what we can and cannot do.

I am against the disparaging remarks of most so-called wine connoisseurs about warm irrigated areas. Without these, the much celebrated export boom would not have gone ahead. We would not have a multi-million dollar industry without Casellas, Bin 65 Chardonnay and Jacobs Creek, the last of which, contrary to what they'd like you to think, is not grown entirely in that little piece of wonderful land called Barossa, but elsewhere, along the Murray River. Some wine varieties – those already grown for centuries in warmer areas of Italy or France – will grow very well in the warmer regions of Australia. At the cost of sounding prophetic, in the next few years we will all enjoy many more unusual wines than has been the case hitherto. Look at the success of the French variety Viognier to get an idea of what's ahead.

a glossary of wines

Following is a list of Italian wine varieties more or less available in Australia at the moment of going to press. There are many plantings going in furiously as I am writing, so the outlook for Italian varieties will certainly be more exciting in the years to come. The purpose of this very brief overview of alternative varieties is to introduce to you names that you may encounter now or in the future and tell you a little about them. For further readings I suggest Nicholas Belfrage's *Barolo to Valpolicella* and *Brunello to Zibibbo*, two serious looks at the wines of the north and the south of Italy. Also by the same author, *Life Beyond Lambrusco*. As this is a book about Italian things, I have excluded, for brevity, French and Spanish varieties such as Viognier, Petit Verdot and Tempranillo. Chalmers Nursery in Euston, near Robinvale, is responsible for an outstanding selection of clones from Italy. The long, but necessary, quarantine process has slowed down the import of varieties, but most are now in the Chalmers' nursery ready to go. The Australian Alternative Varieties Wine Show is held in Mildura annually. The Chairman is distinguished wine personality and grape grower, Robyn Day. Chairman of Judges is Tim White, a wine writer and critic who has ably steered the show over a number of years through the very perilous procedure of adopting guidelines for inclusion of varieties into the show. If you are interested in the Show, it is held annually on the weekend following the famous Melbourne Cup. This is an opportunity to find out what the visionaries are achieving or indeed where they are going wrong.

arneis and cortese

You will find some good examples of this wine from Pizzinis and Crittendens. Arneis is originally from Piedmont in the north-west of Italy. This is without a doubt one of Italy's most characteristic white wines. It was not taken very seriously until recently on account of the fact that Arneis is low yielding and tends to lose acidity rapidly towards maturation. Figures show that Arneis plantings have doubled in the north-west from 1992 to 2002, a sign that winemakers have seen its potential and perhaps have got their heads around it. It is also interesting to note how recent these new plantings are. This fact alone indicates to us that even in old wine-producing countries things change rapidly.

Cortese is another Piedmontese variety grown in Australia. Cortese is interesting because when it gets too cold in Piedmont its acidity is very low. Conversely, it keeps its acidity in warmer years, making it a balanced wine. Sometimes it comes under the name Gavi or Gavi di Gavi. Gavi is the main place where it is grown and Gavi di Gavi simply means Cortese from Gavi. It gets confusing? Yes, but persevere, because that's half the fun.

aglianico

A red wine found in the hills around Naples, especially in the Avellinos area called Irpinia, Caserta and Benevento – and also in the small area north of Potenza, known as Vulture, around the towns of Melfi, Rionero and Barile. Belfrage actually claims that the word barrel (barile in Italian) comes from this town in Basilicata, which was famous for its barrel-making industry. Aglianico is becoming a superstar of Italian wines, next to Nebbiolo and Sangiovese. Once again it worth noting that it is only just not much more than a decade ago when young winemakers and producers got really serious about Aglianico. Although grown in the south, Aglianico does not appear to me to be too big and alcoholic. The better wines are grown at fairly high altitude, mitigating the southern latitude. The hills around Naples can be very cold, with Aglianico ripening fairly late. It seems that Aglianico needs cold nights to keep it from going wild, producing too much sugar and losing balance. Aglianico in many instances – all dependent on DOC rules – is blended with other local red grapes, such as Piedirosso. If you try this wine in Australia – there are many fine examples available from local importers – taste it with a map at hand and demand to know what it has been blended with. Some Australian plantings of Aglianico will soon come to fruition.

barbera

Barbera is found all over Italy, including the south. For some reason this wine has the ability to penetrate a large number of blends. It is probably because it shows heaps of colour and low acidity, making it an ideal blend.

The natural home of Barbera is Piedmont, particularly the Monferrato region. Barbera, although popular in Italy and world over where Italian migrants have settled, is not as 'serious' as its compatriot Nebbiolo. Barbera is a 'drinkable' everyday wine. Some producers have experimented with wood-ageing in new barriques and the general opinion seems to agree that Barbera benefits from time in oak. As usual I have to quote Belfrage, who says that oak seems to impart a nice balance of seriousness and drinkability. Naturally, the old school would prefer ageing in old wood or straight in the bottle. Once again, it is hard to predict what Barbera will do in Australia. There are some good examples here, but if this wine is judged according to the standard measures, it may never be able to deliver. If instead someone aims for a Barbera with pleasant drinking characters, suited to certain food types, then it could have a future.

dolcetto

Another Piedmontese wine, whose name means 'the sweet one', probably referring to the sweetness of its grape, which is really about the balance of sugar, acids and other components. It is an all-purpose wine. In Piedmont there are many types of Dolcetto, therefore when you purchase a bottle of imported Dolcetto look out for the word that accompanies it: is it (Dolcetto) di Diano d'Alba? Di Dogliani? D'Acqui? and so on, each referring to the area or village of provenance.

Popular opinion suggests that Dolcetto d'Asti is superior, indeed, a superstar of Piedmontese wine. Look out for names like Conterno, Azelia, Prunotto, Altare, Rocca, Roddolo, to name but a few; all these megastars produce a Dolcetto d'Asti. In all, this is a very pleasant, everyday wine, low in acid and food friendly.

In Australia one large company has sought to capitalise on the name Dolcetto by making a literally sweet red wine. It may be a legitimate ploy for selling wine, but it has nothing to do with Dolcetto proper. This raises the eternal issue of correct nomenclature. The Italians are not as tough as their Gallic neighbours in protecting the names of their products, but noises have been made about establishing a body for policing the integrity of things Italian.

lagrein

A variety from the area of Bolzano, a city of Alto Adige or, if you prefer, South Tyrol, as this part of the world joined Italy only after World War I. The area in question is high up in the mountains but viticulture is practised on the floor of the valley. Lagrein is mentioned in this book simply because there are a few quirky Australian producers of this variety. I will go on record and risk saying that Australian Lagreins are gamey and rich in colour and flavour, and do not have the bitterness that is typical of the originals. In fact, I have found our Lagreins more rewarding than the imported ones. Look out for Cobaw Ridge, which has won many awards at the Australian Alternative Variety Wine Show.

moscato

There are many sub-varieties of the grape Moscato all over Italy, but it is in Piedmont where Moscato Bianco becomes Moscato d'Asti and simply Asti. Moscato d'Asti is a lovely drink: fragrant, perfumed, lightly bubbly, and low in alcohol. Asti is a less refined example of the same. Whenever you get an Australian-made Moscato or Spumante Moscato, it is usually an extremely tacky imitation of the real thing. When you drink Asti Riccadonna, you drink a passable commercial moscato whose other virtue is said to reside in its ability to make the girls more amenable to a certain type of suggestion.

The success of the brand Riccadonna has obscured the real meaning of the words Asti and moscato. Unwittingly it has become synonymous with a non-serious drink and therefore overlooked by 'proper' wine drinkers. These, however, never fail to be impressed by a reputable Moscato d'Asti, like a Saracco. Committed producers are deadly serious about turning Moscato d'Asti into a cru wine, that is, a single-vineyard wine with a floral bouquet and freshness in the mouth that is as enchanting as it is easy to drink.

A good Moscato d'Asti is *de rigueur* at a Christmas/New Year party with an Italian theme or flavour. Moscato is the natural companion to panettone or to fresh fruit, particularly tropical fruits. It is ideal for pastries with custard. I love it as an aperitif or as that drink after you have had everything else. And it makes a great zabaglione, the Italian dessert par excellence.

Nebbiolo is probably the greatest red wine grape variety in Italy. That is my opinion, at least. It is presented to consumers as Nebbiolo, Barbaresco and Barolo. Actually, in order of importance it should read in reverse. The fact that this variety presents itself in at least three different guises attests to its complex and unpredictable personality.

Nebbiolo is the generic name from wherever, although the label is likely to specify the location – delle Langhe or d'Alba or whatever. When matched to a good producer you have a top wine. In its Barbaresco incarnation it means that it comes from the town of Barbaresco, located a few kilometres east of the Piedmontese town of Alba. In its ultimate incarnation, that of Barolo, the wine is made in the town of Barolo southwest of Alba. And that is only the beginning of the story. It may come from higher up or lower down this or that hilltop; made by this or that producer according to the old-fashioned way or the 'French' way' – with new oak, etc. Families have been known to split down the middle as to which is the right way, with fathers angry at their children for introducing practices hitherto unknown after centuries of solid traditional wine-making practices. Of all the great wines in the world Barolo – and to a lesser extent Barbaresco – is the least understood in Australia, according to my experience. In the thirteen years in the restaurant trade I have sold very few bottles of Barolo, having drunk most of the purchases myself with family or friends. Barolo – and Nebbiolo generally – is a wine with high astringency which takes years of maturation. The old timers like to leave it in the barrel or bottle for a long time, then drink it after many years, often decades, in the bottle. The young modernists prefer to turn it around quickly, adopting techniques usually reserved for other varieties to achieve a more user-friendly drink, rounder and easier to drink and with the flavours of French oak.

Nebbiolo and white truffles conspire to make Piedmont one of the most exciting gastronomic regions of the world. It is surprising to me that most Australians have not been to Piedmont and are not even aware of what it has to offer. If there is a Tuscany of the north it would have to be the Barolo region!

Nebbiolo in Australia – and elsewhere in the world – has shown itself to be just as elusive and problematic as Pinot Noir. However, as Gary Crittenden and the Pizzinis have shown, it is possible to reach for some of its structure and nose. Only perseverance will tell what Nebbiolo's future is here.

Vermentino is said to have originated in Corsica and is now found in Liguria, Tuscany, Sardinia and France, where is it known as Rolle or Malvoisie a Gros Grains. In general it prefers warm coastal areas. It displays, as many other Italian white wines, a certain neutrality of taste, which is ideal for me to accompany Italian white foods, especially seafood, and dishes with a little chilli. In fact, I often wonder if it might not suit certain Asian salads. Vermentino is suitable for wood ageing and I have tasted some good examples in Tuscany. It can also display some oiliness as well as citrus flavours. At the time of writing, Sandro Mosele, winemaker at Kooyong Estate in the Mornington Peninsula, is experimenting with a first batch of Vermentino harvested at Chalmers' Nursery. It will be released under the Murray Darling Collection range. I certainly look forward to this addition to the panorama of new whites, and especially to matching its flavours to Italian food.

Sangiovese or the 'blood of Jove' (Sangue di Giove) is bigger than Ben Hur. It is so successful it can be all things to all people. But while it is found all over Italy, its spiritual home remains Tuscany, where it finds its best expressions.

Sangiovese is the base wine of Chianti, that drink that was made popular in past decades by the raffia-bound 2-litre bottle in which Italian restaurants used to stick a candle. Chianti now is something else, as drinkers of Italian wine have come to notice. It is more palatable as the rules for making it have relaxed considerably. Sangiovese mutates into a clone for another great Tuscan wine, Brunello di Montalcino. In yet another incarnation, Prugnolo gentile, it becomes Vino nobile di Montepulciano. As Morellino, it becomes Morellino di Scansano, and so it goes.

There may be two main Sangiovese: *grosso* and *piccolo*, big and small, referring to berry size. Grosso is actually the better one, although such confusion reigns out there, it is almost impossible to know which is which and which is where. To make matters even more complicated for the inexperienced navigator of Sangiovese is the recent practice of blending it with imported varieties such as Cabernet, Merlot and even Shiraz. It seems that these varieties do well in Tuscany, producing wines of exceptional quality. When Sangiovese is blended with the newcomers, and it is well made, it is called a super-Tuscan, although in some instances it may also be a Chianti, as it is now possible to blend a Chianti brew with the inclusion of 'foreign' guests. In both cases, they are likely to cost a small fortune, but if you want a taste of Italy, it is cheaper than going there.

To my knowledge this variety is not planted in Australia yet, although I believe that an Australian winemaker went over to Italy to make some over there. 'Negro' means dark and 'amaro' means bitter, and not in a negative sense. It is said that the slightly bitter taste is needed to counter the sweet fruit. This is a wine to look out for in the future, as I believe that of all varieties this may do well in hot Australia.

In Italy it is grown almost exclusively in the Apulia region, which is the spur of the peninsula, a rather hot place where loads of grapes are grown for, believe it or not, the French and northern Italian quaff wine industry.

Pinot grigio hardly needs an introduction, as it is becoming increasingly recognised in Australia. Here some confusion emerges between the word *grigio* and the word *gris*, which also means *grigio* in French. The funny thing about this grape is that it is not white but an in-between colour – thus 'grey'.

Gris is grown in Alsace and Germany, whereas the grigio incarnation is Italian, mostly in Trentino and Friuli. In France the wine can be opulent and richly textured, whereas in Italy, it is more of a table wine, not lacking sophistication, but very different in structure and mouth feel. In Australia and in the US winemakers have tended to emulate either the French style or the Italian one. I'd agree with the Australian wine writer Huon Hooke who suggested that since the wine often displays a slightly copper colour, it should be called *ramato*, or copper-like as they sometimes do in the Friuli. Under the name *ramato* there'd be no need for grigio or gris; the difference in style will then be identified by the maker rather than by the name.

Another wine from Apulia, like Negroamaro. Primitivo actually means early, referring to the fact that it can be harvested earlier, even a month earlier than its regional companions. Everyone is happy to accept the fact that Californian Zinfandel is the same grape variety as Primitivo. So, while being an early ripener, it can still produce some sugar, as you'd notice when drinking American Zinfandel or some primitivos from an area called Manduria, in Apulia, which resembles port wine!

Primitivo was not much chop even as recently as a decade ago. I think that the internationalisation of wine is leading the program of discovery of the grape's potential around the globe, unearthing all kinds of possibilities. Experts claim that Primitivo has the ability to produce top wines in warm areas. If a race is on to explore the potential of Primitivo, it may as well include Australia.

risotto al barolo
serves 4

A risotto of the utmost simplicity, but, once again it is dependent on using the best ingredients. This time when you prepare the stock add, besides chicken, some beef bones and beef shin, so that the stock will be strong. I also recommend Parmigiano Reggiano.

40 g butter
40 ml olive oil
1 medium-sized brown onion, peeled and finely diced
200 g Italian risotto rice
250 ml Barolo or a Nebbiolo or a quality Australian red
2 litres Golden Chicken Stock (see page 79), kept simmering
salt and pepper
1 tablespoon butter
Parmigiano Reggiano

Heat the butter and oil in a heavy-based pan and cook the onion until soft. Add the rice and toast the rice by frying it until it has absorbed all the fat. Add a ladleful of red wine and simmer until it evaporates. Now add the stock and red wine, alternating, and making sure you don't add too much wine at a time, as it will cool the risotto down. Stir constantly, until the rice is cooked, but each grain is still slightly firm in the centre. When the last of the stock has been absorbed, the risotto should be a lovely maroon colour. Adjust for salt and pepper and remove from the heat. Add the butter and cheese. Cover for 2 minutes to allow the butter and cheese to amalgamate.

zabaglione with fruits
serves 4

Zabaglione is the oldest trick in the book of Italian desserts. Place some summer fruit – slices of mango or berries – in attractive serving glasses or bowls and pour on the zabaglione. It is delicious. If you like panettone as much as I do, then toast some to accompany.

200 ml Moscato
4 egg yolks
80 g caster sugar
200 ml cream (optional)
a selection of seasonal fruits

Whisk the Moscato, egg yolks and sugar in a stainless steel bowl over a pan of boiling water until the mixture turns pale and fluffy and substantially increases in volume. Remove from the heat and pour over the fruit while still warm.
Alternatively, you can prepare the zabaglione ahead of time, in which case you'll need to stabilise it. Whisk the egg whites to stiff peaks and whip the cream, if using, to soft peaks. Fold the egg whites into the cool zabaglione and then fold in the cream. Refrigerate until ready to use. Serve with your selection of fruit.

sangiovese with peaches
serves 4

Towards the end of summer white peaches start to appear. I prefer the less sweet varieties that seem to dominate at the moment. The old-fashioned peaches also seem a little firmer. Anyway, any good peach will do for this dish. The idea is to marinate them for several hours in a full-bodied sangiovese (or shiraz) with a good dose of sugar. How much sugar is really up to you, so add it gradually until you get the right level of sweetness to balance the wine.

400 ml full-bodied Sangiovese
6 peaches
5 tablespoons caster sugar

Pour the wine into a glass serving bowl and slice in the peaches. Add the sugar, which will fall to the bottom. Stir gently with a spoon until it dissolves. Taste and adjust with a little more sugar (or wine) if need be. Cover the bowl and leave to marinate for several hours. Serve with double cream.

preserves

preserves in all their expressions – jams, marmalades, pickles, chutneys, jardiniere, pastes, jellies – lined up in the pantry are a most enjoyable sight. They represent the bounty of the warmer months and the skilful greed of the provident cook who knows how to store many goodies for the long winter months ahead. Alas, while a few true believers continue the tradition, most people who live in cities and lead a fast life aren't into the art of preserving.

Instead, these days, preserves are sold as commercial products. People like to indulge in the harmless fantasy that some 'mama', or, better still, 'grandma' out there has lovingly created a jar of jam and decorated it with a piece of recycled gingham, but unfortunately in reality that fantasy is the result of a skilled promotion campaign. I am proud to say that, however, a few of us have stuck to our guns, and keep on producing preserves of great integrity and culinary interest with a strong seasonal quality. My friend Maggie Beer does not hesitate to discard a batch of jam she does not like or somehow does

not represent the quality she aspires to. In my kitchen, Lyndall Vandenberg still cuts every orange or nectarine by hand and refuses to cook in pots larger than five litres. Preserves take a fresh product and change it into something else. In effect, there is very little 'preservation' going on. When an orange turns into marmalade, it appears to me that that is a major transformation, rather than an act of preservation. That action is both cultural and gastronomic, and it lifts a vegetable or a fruit to another plane. A pickled mushroom, for instance, has little mushroom flavour left, but the strong flavours of vinegar and spice make it a perfect complement to a pork sausage with a piece of crusty bread. If the product is changed into something else, that 'something else' must stand up on its own in terms of flavour and texture. And this is when you can see the difference between products – the balance of acid to sugar, the colour, the clarity, the consistency and the texture should add to a desirable experience.

I got into preserves because Lyndall joined my kitchen and brought enormous integrity, skill and passion to the job. She had been involved in small catering jobs and felt drawn by the possibilities of preserves when she moved from Western Australia to Mildura for family reasons. This person, unknown to me, walked into my shop and began talking about preserves. I had been working on olive oil and was already leaning towards the idea that Mildura's fruit and vegetable bounty grown in sunshine should end up in a jar. The rest, as they say, was history. Our logo is a mythical creature, part fish, and part bird, reflecting the nature of the Murray River. Our motto is 'Esse Quam Videri', which roughly translates to 'to be rather than to seem'. There is a lot of emphasis on presentation and design when it comes to food in the contemporary, commercial world. A lot of products are stronger in presentation than taste. We wanted to affirm that, for us, content is more important than appearance.

orange marmalade
makes about 1 litre

500 g oranges
1.5 litres water
juice of 1 lemon
850 g white sugar

Wash the oranges to remove any dirt. Cut in half and juice. Reserve the juice. Thinly slice the orange peel, keeping the pith intact. Drop the orange peel into the water, cover and leave to stand overnight.

The next day tip the water and orange peel into a heavy-based, non-reactive shallow pan and bring to the boil. Simmer until the peel is very soft. Add the lemon juice and the reserved orange juice. Return to the boil and simmer for 10 minutes. Add the sugar and stir until completely dissolved. Boil rapidly for about 5 minutes; the marmalade will start to froth up when approaching the setting point.

To test, chill a saucer in the freezer. When cold, place a teaspoon of marmalade onto the saucer and return to the freezer for a moment. The marmalade is ready when it wrinkles as you push your finger through it. Pour into hot sterilised jars and seal. The marmalade will keep in a cool dark place for up to a year.

preserved limes
makes about 700 g

7 limes
100 g rock salt (a good quality salt such as Murray River salt will guarantee the best results)
1 bay leaf
1 tablespoon coriander seeds
extra lime juice
2 tablespoons extra-virgin olive oil

Quarter the limes and press each lime quarter into the salt. Sprinkle a little salt into the bottom of a 700 ml warm sterilised jar. Add the bay leaf. Next, firmly pack into the jar a layer of the limes. Sprinkle with some of the coriander seeds and salt. Repeat until the jar is full. Pour in the extra lime juice so that all the limes are fully submerged. Add the extra-virgin olive oil. Seal.

Store for a minimum of three months before opening. These are best consumed within a year.

antipasto blood oranges
makes about 700 g

1 litre white vinegar
750 g white sugar
4 cardamom, crushed
2 cinnamon quills
2 whole allspice berries, lightly crushed
8 blood oranges
1 cup verjuice

Combine the vinegar and sugar in a heavy-based, non-reactive shallow pan. Stir over a medium heat until the sugar has dissolved. Add the spices. Bring to the boil and simmer gently for 30 minutes or until the spice flavours have strengthened and the vinegar has lost its sharpness.

Meanwhile, slice the blood oranges into very thin rings and carefully add to the preserving liquid with the verjuice. Do not stir as the orange segments will break. Gently shake the pan from time to time to disperse the liquid and oranges. Simmer gently for about 30 minutes or until the liquid has become syrupy and the blood orange rinds are translucent. Carefully pack the blood orange segments into hot sterilised jars, strain the syrup and pour into the jars. Seal and store for a minimum of a month before opening so that the flavours develop. This preserve will be at its best after six months. Eat within a year of making.

1 x 1 kg pickled ox tongue
2 onions, peeled and quartered
1 stick celery, cut into long lengths
1 medium-sized carrot, cut into long lengths
Antipasto Blood Oranges (see page 245)

blood orange segments and ox tongue | serves 6 and more

Place the tongue, onions, celery and carrot in a large pot, cover with water and simmer for 2 hours or until the tongue is soft.
Remove from the pot and use a sharp knife to carefully peel away the outer skin. Carve into slices and serve with the pickled blood oranges, a mound of mashed potato and perhaps a dollop of tangy salsa verde. It is best served as a part of a large bollito misto dish.

apple and vanilla bean jam
makes about 750 g

1 kg apples (Pink Ladies are best)
juice of 1 lemon
1 vanilla bean
750 g white sugar

Peel and core the apples. Retain a quarter of the cores and tie them in a muslin bag – they provide extra pectin which helps the jam to set. Cut the apples into chunks.
In a heavy-based, non-reactive shallow pan combine the apples, apple cores in their bag and the lemon juice. Cook gently until the apples start to break down.
Split the vanilla bean in half and scrape out the seeds. Add the pod and seeds to the apple mixture and stir to combine. Add the sugar and stir until it dissolves. Raise the heat to high and cook for about 5 minutes, watching carefully to see that it doesn't catch and burn.
After about 5 minutes the jam should start to reach its setting point. Tip the pan to one side and to see if a jelly has begun to form on the bottom of the pan. If so, the jam is ready. (You can also test on a chilled saucer, see page 245.)
Remove the apple cores and the vanilla pod and spoon into hot sterilised jars. Seal and store for up to 6 months.

quince paste
makes 2 kg

8 quince
juice of 1 lemon
½ cup water
white sugar

Peel, core and chop the quince. Retain a quarter of the cores.
In a heavy-based, non-reactive shallow pan combine the quince, quince cores and the lemon juice with the water. Cook gently until the quince are soft, about 30 minutes.
Tip the mixture into a food processor and blend until smooth. The cores will not break down completely; however, this gives the paste some texture.
Weigh the quince mixture and for every 1 kg of quince add 75 g sugar. Return to the pot. Dissolve the sugar by stirring over a medium heat. Once the sugar has dissolved, cook the quince paste over a gentle heat for 2–3 hours, stirring from time to time to make sure it doesn't stick to the bottom of the pan. The paste will change to a beautiful ruby colour, and is ready when the paste starts to leave the sides of the pan as you stir.
Spray a shallow, non-reactive baking tray with oil and line with baking paper, making sure it reaches up and over the sides at either end. Pour the paste into the prepared tray and leave to set overnight at room temperature.
Grasp the baking paper at either end and gently lift the paste out of the tray. Turn onto a drying rack and peel away the baking paper. Leave for several days to dry out.
Store in an airtight container in a cool dry place. The quince paste will keep for 12 months.

caramelised figs
makes 2 kg

Great with antipasto or paired with gorgonzola cheese.

3 cups white sugar
1 cup water
1 cup balsamic vinegar
3 cinnamon quills
2 star anise
1 vanilla bean
1 kg figs

Put the sugar, water and vinegar in a non-reactive saucepan and heat gently to dissolve the sugar. Bring to the boil, and add the spices once the sugar has completely dissolved. Simmer for 30 minutes to develop the flavours.
Gently add the figs to the syrup and poach very, very gently for 2 hours, or until the syrup has thickened and been absorbed into the figs.
Preheat the oven to 120°C. Carefully transfer the figs to a wire rack, placed in a baking dish to drain.
Transfer the dish to the oven and bake for 3–4 hours, or until the figs no longer expel liquid and have caramelised.
Cool and store in an airtight container for up to 3 months.

pickled eggplant

makes about 750 g

2 kg eggplant
3 tablespoons dried oregano
3 red chillies, sliced lengthwise
    into quarters
3 cloves garlic, peeled and sliced
8 tablespoons salt
white vinegar
olive oil

Peel the eggplant and cut lengthwise into slices 2–3 mm thick. Cut these slices into long strips 2–3 mm wide. Working quickly to avoid them discolouring, place a third of the eggplant strips into a plastic container and sprinkle with 1 tablespoon of oregano, 1 chilli, 1 garlic clove and 2 tablespoons of salt. Toss together. Repeat the process until all the ingredients have been used. Finally, sprinkle 1 tablespoon of salt over the top of the eggplant mixture.

Take a second plastic container which will fit snuggly into the first container. Place it inside a plastic bag and fill the container with water. Place the second container into the first container and spread the bag over the walls of the first container. Weight both containers with a heavy object. Leave in a cool place for 48 hours. The salting and weighing is to extract water from the vegetables to be pickled.

After 48 hours, remove the second container and squeeze the excess water from the eggplant. Discard the water. Return the eggplant to the first container and add enough white vinegar to cover the eggplant completely. Cover with the plastic container and bag and leave for 48 hours.

Tip the eggplant into a colander and squeeze out as much excess vinegar as you can. Pack into warm sterilised jars. Pour on enough olive oil to completely cover the eggplant, making sure there are not little bubbles or trapped air pockets. Seal and store in the refrigerator for up to a month.

cotechino with pickled eggplant
serves 6

Cotechino is available from specialist Italian butchers in all the major capital cities. The dish is pictured opposite.

1 x 1 kg cotechino sausage
1 stick celery
2 onions, studded with a dozen cloves
1 carrot
Pickled Eggplant (see page 249)

Place all the ingredients in a large saucepan, cover with cold water and simmer for 1½ hours until soft. Slice the cotechino and serve on mashed potatoes with salsa verde and the pickled eggplant. You'll only need a small amount of the eggplant with each mouthful.

tomato, capsicum and eggplant relish
makes 500 g

This sweet and spicy relish is great with smoked ham and other salted meats.

1 medium-sized eggplant
salt
1 tablespoon olive oil
1 onion, finely chopped
2 teaspoons ground coriander
2 teaspoons ground cumin
2 cardamom pods, crushed
1 cinnamon stick
2 red capsicum, seeded and chopped
2 large ripe tomatoes, chopped
200 ml red wine vinegar
½ cup brown sugar
½ cup white sugar
2 red chillies, finely chopped
2 tablespoons muscatels

Peel and chop the eggplant, sprinkle with salt and leave to stand for 30 minutes.
Heat the oil in a frying pan and sauté the onion. Add the spices and cook for a few minutes over a low heat. Add the capsicum and cook for a further 10 minutes or until soft.
Squeeze the water from the eggplant and add to the pan with the remaining ingredients. Cook over a low heat for 1 hour, or until the mixture has thickened and cooked down. Pour into hot sterilised jars and seal. The relish is best eaten within 3 months.

nectarine or peach jam
makes about 750 g

1 kg nectarines or yellow-fleshed peaches, firm and ripe
juice and zest of 1 lemon
750 g white sugar

Chop the fruit into small chunks and place in a heavy-based non-reactive pan with the lemon juice. Cook gently until the fruit is very soft and has begun to break down. Be careful to cook off any excess liquid.
Add the lemon zest and cook for a few minutes. Add the sugar and stir to dissolve. Increase the heat and bring the fruit to the boil. Keep a close eye on the pan as the jam burns easily; stir from time to time.
Cook for about 15 minutes or until the jam has thickened.
Spoon into hot sterilised jars and seal. Best eaten within 6 months.

These are amazing with panna cotta or with breakfast porridge.

2 cups white sugar

4 cups water

3 large or 6 small quince

1 vanilla bean, split

1 star anise

2 cinnamon quills

quince poached in spiced syrup | makes enough to serve 4

Put the sugar and water into a large saucepan and heat gently until the sugar has dissolved.
Peel and core the quince and set aside the peel and cores. Cut each quince into 8 pieces and place in a large non-reactive baking tray. Add the spices.

Cover the quince pieces with a piece of muslin and scatter the peel and cores on top – these will add flavour and colour.

Pour the sugar syrup into the baking tray and cover the whole thing with aluminium foil. Cook gently for 3–4 hours, or until the quince soften and turn a beautiful ruby colour.

Carefully lift away the muslin with the peel and cores. Transfer the quince to a container and pour on the syrup. Cover and refrigerate for up to 1 month. Alternatively, put the quince pieces into hot sterilised jars. Seal and boil them, fully submerged in a water bath, for 15 minutes. These are then best consumed within 6 months.

Conversions & Equivalents

Oven Temperatures

Celsius	Fahrenheit	Description
140°C	275° F	very cool
150°C	300° F	cool
170°C	325° F	warm
180°C	350° F	moderate
190°C	375° F	fairly hot
200°C	400° F	fairly hot
220°C	425° F	hot
230°C	450° F	very hot
240°C	475° F	extremely hot

Liquid Measures

1 metric teaspoon	5 ml	
1 metric tablespoon	20 ml	
1 US tablespoon	15 ml	
¼ metric cup	60 ml	2 fl oz
½ metric cup	125 ml	4 fl oz
1 metric cup	250 ml	8 fl oz
4 metric cups	1 litre	2 pints

Millilitres	Fluid Ounces
30 ml	1 fl oz
60 ml	2 fl oz
75 ml	3 fl oz
125 ml	4 fl oz
150 ml	5 fl oz (¼ pint)
250 ml	8 fl oz
275 ml	10 fl oz (½ pint)
570 ml	1 pint
720 ml	1¼ pints
870 ml	1½ pints
1 litre	2 pints

Tablespoons/cups	Imperial	Grams
1 pinch (less than ⅛ teaspoon)		0.5 g
1 dash (3 drops to ¼ teaspoon)		1.25 g
1 teaspoon		5.0 g
1 tablespoon	½ oz	15 g
2 tablespoons	1 oz	30 g
¼ cup	2 oz	60 g
½ cup	4 oz	120 g
1 cup	8 oz	250 g
2 cups	16 oz (1 lb)	500 g

Note: The US tablespoon is 15 g and the metric measure for a tablespoon is 20 g.

Solid Measures

Grams	Ounces	Grams	Ounces
30 g	1 oz	270 g	9 oz
50 g	1½ oz	300 g	10 oz
60 g	2 oz	330 g	11 oz
100 g	3 oz	360 g	12 oz
120 g	4 oz	390 g	13 oz
150 g	5 oz	400 g	14 oz
180 g	6 oz	450 g	15 oz
200 g	7 oz	500 g	16 oz (1 lb)
250 g	8 oz	1 kg	2 lb

Index